PRAISE FOR
Breakthrough Intuition

"To say I am impressed with Rosemary Ellen Guiley's book would be an understatement. In reading it I found myself lamenting that a book of this caliber was not available back in the sixties when I first began to refine my own intuitive abilities. Rosemary is more than a researcher. She is an accomplished intuitive counselor, who had to overcome serious doubts about her own abilities before she could explore the scope of intuition itself and its link to the soul. Her cautions and advice, not to mention exercises for the beginner as well as the more experienced, are superb."

—P.M.H. ATWATER, LH.D.,
author of *Beyond the Light* and *Future Memory*

"Rosemary Guiley's considerable strengths: the ability to organize material; the gift of being able to write about sometimes difficult subjects in a direct, clear, compelling manner; and best of all, the deep well of her own exceptional experiences from which she draws informs her writing with an authenticity missing from many books. There are many titles available on pyschic ability and intuition, but even if you've read them all, be sure not to miss this one."

—RHEA A. WHITE,
director of Exceptional Human Experience Network

"This is an outstanding guide to the use of intuition in all aspects of our lives, both in theory and practice. The exercises for developing intuition are clear, effective, and safe. This is the all-around best guide for anyone who wants to begin activating his or her intuitive ability."

—JOHN WHITE, author of *The Meeting of Science and Spirit* and *What Is Enlightenment?*

"You can be assured that the keys to intuition presented by Rosemary Ellen Guiley will work magic in your life—even if you do not believe this could happen for you. Rosemary herself did not believe she was intuitive when she first embarked on an inner journey that has transformed her life and thousands of others who have been touched by her books. I can attest, based on my own personal experiences, that potent possibilities are available to those who are willing to experiment with the methods presented herein. I highly recommend this book."

—JEFFREY MISHLOVE, PH.D.,
author of *The Roots of Consciousness*

"A wide-ranging, multifaceted compilation that pulls together and offers a rich array of exercises and approaches to developing intuitive ability. There is something here for everyone."

—... ARSTEK,
... *th Sense*

N 2 0 200

Breakthrough Intuition

How to Achieve a Life

of Abundance by Listening

to the Voice Within

ROSEMARY
ELLEN GUILEY

BERKLEY BOOKS, NEW YORK

B

A Berkley Book
Published by The Berkley Publishing Group
A division of Penguin Putnam Inc.
375 Hudson Street
New York, New York 10014

Copyright © 2001 by Visionary Living, Inc.
Cover design by Jill Boltin
Text design by Tiffany Kukec

PRINTING HISTORY
Berkley trade paperback edition / March 2001

The Penguin Putnam Inc. World Wide Web site address is
http://www.penguinputnam.com

Library of Congress Cataloging-in-Publication Data

Guiley, Rosemary.
    Breakthrough intuition : how to achieve a life of abundance by listening to the
voice within / Rosemary Ellen Guiley.—Berkley trade pbk. ed.
        p.   cm.
    Includes bibliographical references.
    ISBN 0-425-17655-X
    1. Parapsychology. 2. Intuition. I. Title.

BF1031 .G78 2001
131—dc21

                                                                        00-050790

PRINTED IN THE UNITED STATES OF AMERICA

10 9 8 7 6 5 4 3 2 1

Acknowledgments

I AM GRATEFUL FOR THE INSPIRATION AND HELP FROM MY friends Carol Adrienne, who wrote the foreword to this book, and Nancy Rosanoff, both talented intuitives and teachers. I would also like to thank my dear friend Rev. Toni G. Boehm for her insights on "spiritual cues," and for her permission to adapt an exercise on "Walking the Labyrinth" from our collaborative effort, *Inner Visioning*.

A special thanks to Connie Bowen, author and artist of beautiful children's books of affirmations, for sharing some of her personal experiences that so aptly illustrate the principles of the blessings that flow from living intuitively.

I am indebted to the healing work of Mietek and Margaret Wirkus, whose wonderful classes on energy healing taught me a great deal about subtle energy and inspired several of the exercises in the Keys.

Contents

PART III: Using Your Intuition

Foreword

I WILL NEVER FORGET THE FIRST TIME I HEARD ROSEMARY
Guiley give her presentation on the presence of angels. We were
both lecturing at the annual conference of the International Institute of Integral Human Sciences in Montreal. Rosemary talked
eloquently about a host of startling true-life anecdotes of angelic
presence. I remember one such story of a woman whose car slid
out of control on an icy road during a snowstorm. As the car
careened into a steep ditch, she felt invisible hands yank the steering wheel, preventing the car from flipping onto its side. She was
saved from certain injury, possibly even death. Such experiences
may indeed be the presence of our guardian angels.

Not only did Rosemary share with us that day many other
such instances of the presence of an inner request for help or an
inner knowing that was crucial for a decision, she also visually
illustrated the presence of angels through a stunning series of
painted angels throughout history—from medieval depictions,
through the Italian and Northern Renaissance painters, to present
day artistic expressions. To further drive home the magnificence
of angelic spiritual presence, Rosemary had selected a number of

extremely moving pieces of classical music, which transported the audience right into the angelic realms. I was also struck by her comment that some people believe that the occurrence of the number twenty-two is a sign that angels are present. Twenty-two has always been a significant number to me both personally and professionally as a numerologist, and I am delighted to see it in this light.

Breakthrough Intuition: How to Achieve a Life of Abundance by Listening to the Voice Within, is organized with the same care for giving an *experience* of the intangible, but very real, movement of intuition. Intuition is our own personal guidance system and connection to something greater than ourselves. In the last decade, intuition has become a very popular idea, as if it were newly discovered, and something to be developed as a tool for a more fulfilling life. In fact, intuition is always quietly present within us, and sometimes startlingly so. In my own review of the past events of my life, I have been able to isolate some very important intuitions that at the time seemed nothing more than rather nagging thoughts.

The first intuition, which I now see as the very beginning of my spiritual path, was the idea that I should change my name after my divorce in 1969. For months, this thought would keep returning, but I did nothing about taking action. It persisted. I realize now that certain other events had to take place before the intuition could work its magic. At that time, I had moved on impulse from California, to Santa Fe, New Mexico, following a one-week's vacation there. I had come home from the vacation, quit my job in the Bay Area, and moved myself and my two children there, not knowing a soul. After a series of synchronicities that opened many doors, I kept hearing from my new friends that I should meet another friend of theirs, Ruth Drayer. I finally did meet Ruth at a party and casually mentioned (for some unconscious reason!) that I had been thinking of changing my name. It was Ruth who said, "Oh, you should use numerology to harmonize a new name with your birthday." She offered to do a numerology chart for me, and we worked out what is now my present name. When I discovered this system of reading character and destiny from a person's name and birth date, I was completely fascinated. My study of numerology was the beginning of the work I now do today, even though it plays a lesser part in my writing and teaching than it did in the beginning. My small but persistent thought to change my name actually was the key to opening the door to my destiny as a teacher. Who knew?

Following that event, another intuition, or persistent thought, came into my head. I knew without a doubt that my time in Santa Fe was now over. I also knew that the next step for me was to return to graduate school, even though, ironically, I had absolutely no desire to go back to school, and no idea of where to go or what to study. I knew I was interested in metaphysical and psychological subjects, but as this was 1971, there were few humanistic and transpersonal psychology programs yet available. Again, I had to follow my intuition to take me where I needed to go. I had to trust that something was working through me.

I took a few small steps. Some things worked out beautifully and seemed to give me the go-ahead. I entered graduate school in Sonoma County, California, but then hit a brick wall. I could not find even one part-time job to support myself and my children while I attended school. What to do? My intuition said, stop and wait for a while. Give up. So I took what seemed like a backward step and took an office job back in Berkeley. A year went by until my best friend, after returning from a year traveling around the world, called to tell me she had found a graduate program in archetypal psychology that she was very excited about at the college in Sonoma. She had had an intuitive vision in Europe that she would find a certain farmhouse to live in, in a landscape that she saw with rolling brown hills and cows. She and her husband eventually did find this exact farmhouse in Petaluma, California. The vision had also included a blackboard with signs and symbols on it, and she intuitively felt this new program she had found was the next step for her, and that both of us should attend.

After that, the synchronicities flowed again, and I intuitively found the right place to live and several part-time jobs. The program was exactly what I was now interested in. From this foundation, my path has continued to unfold.

I have learned several things about the intuitive process. First, intuition is persistent. You hear it in the middle of the night, at stoplights, in line at the grocery store, while talking to a friend on the phone, or when you're reflecting on a decision. It's a quiet sense of direction or an idea about an action to take. Usually you don't know how to accomplish it exactly, but you will continue to get further guidance if you take a small step in that direction. Your inner discriminating function draws upon both intuitive and rational processes. Intuition and rational thinking work beautifully together if you honor both of them. Sometimes intuition may come with a bit of fear, because usually it's pushing you out of your comfort zone a little. So don't automatically assume that the fear is a "no." It just may be a sign that this *is* new territory, therefore it's prudent to amplify all your senses, to stay very aware of your process, but go ahead and explore this new territory for the growth it offers you. Don't wait for absolute "clarity" before taking action. Look within yourself and ask, "Am I asking for clarity, or am I asking for a *guarantee* that my goals will work out just as I have envisioned them today?"

I think it's important to know that following our intuition may not always take us to the conclusion that we expected. We may even feel that the intuition to go ahead with something seemed to bring a negative outcome. However, this is the point on the spiritual path when we are asked to take a larger view of the happening. Ask yourself, "Even though my intuition seemed to be off here, did I not learn something of even greater depth than what I had expected?" I don't know the answer. But you will . . . intuitively. The key is to ask for what you want, focus on what you want, and then go in the direction that *feels* best.

Rosemary Ellen Guiley is a wonderful guide in the realm of the invisible. I hope you enjoy this clear and inspiring book as much as I did.

—Carol Adrienne, Ph.D., author of *The Purpose of Your Life, Finding Your Place in the World Using Synchronicity, Intuition, and Uncommon Sense*, and coauthor with James Redfield of *The Celestine Prophecy: An Experiential Guide*

Introduction

ONCE UPON A TIME I DID NOT CONSIDER MYSELF PARTICU-
larly intuitive. Today I teach others how to develop their own
intuitive gifts. The transition was surprisingly easy. Once I accepted the fact that we are all *naturally* intuitive, I was able to
develop my own ability. It was like a flower opening with a little
watering, fertilizer, and encouragement.

Most people think of themselves as intuitively blocked. They
unwittingly shut themselves off from a tremendous source of
guidance, wisdom, insight, creativity, and healing. I feel a great
deal of joy when I'm able to show them how keenly intuitive they
really are. They discover a whole new dimension to living. Intuition enhances everything we do—our jobs, our relationships, our
self-esteem, our creativity, our health—and our ability to dream
bold visions of the future. When we allow our intuition to work
for us, we are better equipped to make good decisions, for everything from driving a particular route to making career changes to
investing our money to involvements with other people. We are
more likely to have great ideas—and know how to act on them—
and feel more energized and full of vitality.

Is intuition psychic? Yes. Is it spiritual? Very. Is it mystical? Certainly.

Does everyone have intuition?

Absolutely.

We cannot approach intuition as something that can be kept in a separate little box, apart from the rest of our life. The very nature, the very purpose of intuition is to improve our lives *holistically*. Intuition opens us up to our own deep and profound wisdom that can guide us in all ways, from our jobs to our homes and relationships to our self-esteem to our sense of place in the world and in the universe.

"Psychic" has become more accepted in the mainstream, but many of us still are uncomfortable with terms like "spiritual" and "mystical." We have the odd notion that in order to be spiritual or mystical, we have to spend a lot of time sitting in church pews, or we must withdraw to monasteries or become another Mother Teresa.

Everything in life has a spiritual component—and sometimes a mystical one, too. When you give or receive love, that's spiritual. When you do a favor for someone, that's spiritual. When you express your creativity, that's spiritual. When you beautify your home by cleaning it or decorating it, that's spiritual. When you do your job well, that's spiritual. When you appreciate the order and beauty of nature or sense the presence of the Divine, you have touched on the mystical.

We can't avoid being spiritual. We are souls in bodies, incarnate and playing out a purpose in the cosmos. We are born spiritual. We have an inborn sense of the mystical. We are naturally intuitive. We are naturally psychic.

All we have to do is open the door to our birthright.

I meet people who want to be intuitive, but they want to treat their intuition like a widget. "Okay, I need to be intuitive now to make this decision, so I'll get my widget out." Yes, you can train your intuition to jump through a few hoops for you, but sooner or later you will have a hard time preventing your intuition from spilling over into the whole of your life. And why wouldn't you want your intuition functionally in your whole life, anyway? Your intuition guides you in the unfolding of your highest and best potential. Ultimately, you stand to become a better person. Happier. More fulfilled. More self-confident. And more filled with those spiritual qualities such as love, kindness, patience, compassion, generosity, and so forth.

You will benefit from this book if:

• *You need some new direction in life*. All of us go through periods in which we feel overwhelmed by problems, or we're being pulled in too many directions, or we can't seem to get a clear head about making decisions. You can take control of your life now by putting your intuition to work for you.

• *You wish to improve your performance at work*. Whether you are self-employed, starting up a new business, or working in a large organization, you can shine with ideas, visionary thinking, and creative problem-solving. The intuition-building exercises in this book will show you how.

• *You have a hard time making up your mind*. You struggle with decisions, engaging in endless vacillation, weighing of pros and cons, and fence-sitting. Once decisions are made, you engage in endless second-guessing. Stop! Your intuition will help you see things more clearly. You can make sound decisions more quickly and free up time and energy to move ahead.

• *Things often seem to go wrong for you*. You find yourself singing the same glum refrains, "The story of my life!" or "This always happens to me." You will change those refrains to a happier tune when you learn to understand and trust the guidance of your intuition.

• *You want to be more creative*. Do you feel that you're not using your full potential, but you're not sure what to do about it? There is tremendous creativity within all of us. You don't necessarily need to drop what you're doing and take up something radically new. Your intuition will show you how to unfold like a blossoming flower.

• *Things are going well but you'd like for them to go even better.* Our intuition is constantly guiding us toward achieving our highest fulfillment in terms of abundance, success, satisfaction, love, health, and spiritual development.

• *You picked up this book.* Your intuition guided you to here. The message from your Higher Self is, "I can help you find what you need. I want to help you."

So start now. You'll find the ninety-four exercises in this book easy to do. I know from my own experience that if self-improvement exercises are too complicated, they don't get done. The exercises here are simple, solid, basic, proven, and very effective. Some will be familiar to you, others will be new. Try them all. They are designed to acquaint you with the various nuances of your intuition and help you to gain confidence in the information you receive. Everyone experiences the intuition in his or her own unique way. Your intuition will tell you which ones work best for you. You will develop your own personal intuitive style.

Part III of this book, "Using Your Intuition," will show you how your intuition can give you practical help with self-improvement, relationships, work, creativity, prosperity, health, and visionary thinking.

A more abundant and satisfying life awaits you. Our intuition is one of our best tools for building an abundant and satisfying life. Take what's naturally yours and fulfill your dreams.

—Rosemary Ellen Guiley

▣ PART I

Your Intuitive Consciousness

Chapter One

Intuition Is Your Birthright

Every day, intuition saves people from inconvenience, injury, and even death. And it may have even saved the world from nuclear disaster.

In 1983, the world came perilously close to nuclear war. Only a few people knew then how narrowly we missed an exchange of nuclear missiles between the United States and the Soviet Union. The story did not reach the public until October 1998, when it was reported by news agencies around the world.

In the weeks following the shooting down of a Korean Air jumbo jet by the Soviet Union, tension was high. The Boeing 747 passenger jet had strayed into Soviet airspace and been shot down by the military, killing everyone on board.

On one night in September 1983, a Russian army lieutenant colonel and software engineer named Stanislav Petrov was on duty at a military satellite surveillance center near Moscow. The surveillance provided early warning of any incoming missiles. Just after midnight, Petrov's computer screen suddenly flashed the words, MISSILE ATTACK. A piercing alarm sounded. The system indicated that a missile had been launched from a U.S. base.

Petrov's orders were to immediately notify superiors. If missiles were en route, a counterattack would be launched right away. Every second counted.

Stunned, Petrov hesitated, weighing the terrible consequences of confirming an attack. He then noticed that ground-based radar did not indicate missiles had been launched. Within minutes he concluded that the satellite system had given a false alarm.

But a new alarm sounded, indicating four more missiles had been launched from the U.S. base. What if he was wrong? Petrov held firm to his conclusion. It was, in part, he said, a "gut feeling" that no one really wanted to start a nuclear war.

Petrov reported the alarm as false. A subsequent investigation revealed that sunlight reflecting off clouds had been the culprit.

"Petrov's decision to disobey procedure was intuitive," stated the BBC in its 1998 report about the incident.[1]

The story illustrates how intuition often works: it grabbed Petrov with a visceral "gut feeling" and ran counter to the prevailing data. As a result, a devastating mistake was avoided.

Intuition played a role in one of the most famous disasters of history: the sinking of the luxury liner *Titanic*. Intuition did not avert the disaster, but it did save lives.

A few days before the *Titanic* was scheduled to depart Southampton, England, on its maiden voyage to New York in April 1912, American business magnate J. Pierpont Morgan suddenly canceled his first-class ticket, deciding that it was better for him not to go. He wasn't alone.

Other passengers canceled their tickets, too. Some experienced uneasy dreams about the ship sinking. Some decided it wasn't a good idea to travel, without knowing exactly why. Some were diverted by unexpected events that conflicted with their plans for their trip.

And some inadvertently lost their chance to sail. A group of twenty-two stokers found themselves late in getting to the dock. They raced up to the ship, but the irate captain told them the ship was going to leave without them. It did, leaving them puzzled and upset over losing their jobs. Days later, their distress turned to profound shock and relief when news came that the *Titanic* had struck an iceberg and sunk. Killed were 1502 of the 2207 passengers aboard. It was one of the worst maritime disasters of peacetime.

The disaster of the *Titanic* would have been much worse if the ship had carried a full load of passengers. In fact, it sailed with only 58 percent of its passenger capacity. Why did the most prestigious and heavily promoted ocean liner of its day attract such a relatively small crowd of passengers? Why wasn't it fully booked on its grand maiden voyage? And why did some people not follow through on their plans to sail?

The answer is intuition. You can also call it premonition, precognition, psychic foresight, hunch, or gut instinct, but they're all terms describing the same faculty: the ability to know something that cannot be explained by the facts at hand. For some people who'd planned to travel on the *Titanic*, their intuition had spoken clearly: they had had nightmarish dreams about the ship sinking that seemed very realistic, or they had had profound unease about going. For others, the intuition had been more indirect: there was no inkling of disaster, but they'd felt strongly guided by some inner voice or prompting to change their plans. And for others, events of the world in the form of synchronicity intervened: unexpected conflicts of time, such as happened to the group of stokers who were "inexplicably" tardy for the big day.

There have been many cases of intuitive guidance that have prevented people from being injured or losing their lives in accidents and disasters. You hear about them every day in the news: "I don't know, something just told me not to get on the plane. . . ." "I decided not to take the same route to work, so I was late and that meant I missed being in the bomb blast. . . ." "I decided to leave earlier than I'd planned, so I missed the accident that tied up the freeway for two hours. . . ." and so on. A study done some years ago of passenger loads on American trains that had accidents showed a remarkable drop-off in average numbers of passengers on the days of the accidents. Conclusion: *something* prompted people to alter their plans or miss the trains.[2]

That "something" is intuition.

But our intuition works for us in more than diverting disaster. Most of us, hopefully, will never face such dire circumstances as described above. Yet our intuition still works for us all the time, pushing us, pulling us, guiding us, encouraging us, and warning us about everything—yes *everything*—that goes on in our lives. The intuition is behind the impulse to call someone, the inspiration to try something novel, the decision to take a risk, the solution to a problem, the right words to say, and the seemingly impulsive act to take. Our intuition works for us on the big things and the small things in life.

In preparation for a trip to Japan, I bought some gifts for the people I would be seeing there. Gift-giving is an important social custom in Japan. I purchased three angel music boxes for three women I had met on a previous trip there, and whom I would be meeting together again on this trip. Each music box was slightly different. One had a pink angel playing a harp. One had a blue angel playing a trumpet. And one had an angel taking the hand of a child. Each played a different melody. Did it matter which one I gave to which person? I didn't know any of the women well. I wrapped the angels up and put names on them.

When the gifts were opened, it turned out that each woman had the "right" angel. The lady whose favorite color was pink received the pink angel. The lady whose favorite color was blue received the blue angel. The song played by the angel with a child was a favorite of the lady who received that music box. They were pleased and surprised at how personal their gifts were. How had I known those things, they wanted to know. I smiled and said, "I think the angels told me."

How did it work out that way? Was I just lucky when I decided who would get which angel?

I simply let my intuition choose for me. As I held each angel, I allowed myself to "feel" a name that went with it.

My intuition has worked for me in countless ways, making decisions major and minor. I have learned through trial and error that if I override intuition, things invariably don't work out the way I had anticipated. We've all been in the same position: We've found ourselves saying, "I *knew* I should/shouldn't have. . . ."

Everyone is born with intuitive ability. Most people, however, regard themselves as intuitively blocked or not gifted. Thus, they unwittingly shut themselves off from a tremendous natural and inborn source of guidance, wisdom, insight, creativity, and healing. When you discover how keenly intuitive you really are, a whole new dimension of living is revealed. Intuition enhances everything we do—our jobs, our relationships, our self-esteem, our creativity, our health—and our ability to dream bold visions of the future. When we allow our intuition to work for us, we are better equipped to make good decisions, for everything from driving a particular route to making career changes to investing our money to involvements with other people. We are more likely to have great ideas—and know how to act on them—and feel more energized and full of vitality.

All of us can reach within and find this gift and develop it. What's more, it's easier to do than you might think. The exercises in this book will show you how.

Self Test

You are intuitive if (check all that apply):

- You have "hunches" or "gut feelings" about how something will work out

- You are prompted by your "good judgment"

- You "get" a "lucky break"

- You inexplicably "know" something

- You have a "feeling" that something will happen

- Your dreams give you guidance

- You find yourself in the right place at the right time

- Your "guesses" turn out to be uncannily accurate

- You feel guided by higher powers

- You have flashes of insight in which things seem crystal clear

- You feel strong impulses to do something that runs contrary to reason

If you answered yes to even one statement—if you can only think of one episode in your entire life—then you've affirmed your basic, inborn ability to be intuitive. That ability may not be readily apparent to you now, but with a little encouragement will become a strong and powerful force in your life.

You are intuitive *and* smart if:

You *act* on any of the above

How will intuition help you in your life? Count the ways:

- Plan your day more effectively to make the best use of your time

- Make decisions big and small without fence-sitting, vacillating, and second-guessing

- Sense the moods and feelings of others so you can make appropriate responses

- Sense the best timing and approach for relating to others, such as asking for favors, mending strained relationships, and improving personal communications

- Motivate others

- Handle confrontations

- Improve your health and the health of others

- Find lost objects

- Feel more comfortable about risk-taking

- Stimulate more creativity, energy, and vitality

- Improve your self-confidence and self-image

You can enjoy all these benefits and more by letting your intuition be your guide.

Chapter Two

Your Psychic Sense and Auric Blueprint

Is THERE A DIFFERENCE BETWEEN BEING INTUITIVE AND PSY-chic? Is it possible to be one without the other?

The answer to both questions is that it is very difficult to separate the two.

The term "psychic" comes from the Greek word *psyche,* which means "of the soul." It refers to our inner state of being. Psychic ability thus springs from the very core of our being. It truly is a gift—a gift from the Creator, the Source of All Being, a resource to help us realize our full potential as human beings and as souls.

Intuition and psi both involve a knowing that comes from beyond the five senses, yet makes use of the senses in order to convey information. Harold Sherman, a pioneer in research of psi, described the psi faculties as part of our intuitive level of con-sciousness. Development of the psi faculty is necessary in order to reach our cosmic consciousness level, in which our total being becomes fused with the God Presence.

Psychic faculties function in a variety of ways and overlap with one another. They are all part of the intuitive experience. Here are descriptions:

- *Precognition* is direct knowledge or perception of the future, obtained through extraordinary means. Precognition is the most frequently reported of all extrasensory perception experiences. According to studies, it occurs most often (60 to 70 percent) in dreams. Precognition also occurs in waking visions, sudden thoughts, and the inner voice. Most experiences of precognition happen within one to two days of an event. A small minority can occur months, even years, before the actual event takes place.

Everyone has at least one experience of precognition during life. Such episodes may involve traumatic events. The emotional intensity surrounding trauma seems to break through the normal barriers most of us have to accessing information from the future or distant places.

Actually, we experience "little precognitions" all the time. For example, you may have a sudden and certain feeling that you will encounter a particular person, whom you have not seen in a long time, later in the day. You shrug it off as imagination—and then run into that very person, just as you "saw."

Precognition is the basis for divination, prophecy, and prediction, which have been practiced by all societies around the world since ancient times. Traditionally, individuals with natural, exceptional psychic gifts, or who had been specially trained, served in official capacities to advise heads of state about the future. To stimulate precognition, they induced trance or read the random patterns of nature—such as clouds, the flights of birds, or rising smoke—or tossed objects, such as stones or bones. These methods and tools do not in themselves contain precognitive information, but are a means to open the inner intuitive/psychic faculty. You may find some tools described in the exercises in this book useful yourself.

- *Premonition* is a first cousin to precognition that is generally experienced as a foreboding or warning. Premonitions are often vague and more generalized, such as a "feeling" that something unpleasant may happen. Premonitions probably were behind many of the canceled plans to sail on the *Titanic*.

▪ *Telepathy* is mind-to-mind communication of thoughts, feelings, ideas, sensations, and mental images. Telepathy can occur between any two persons, or even among a group of persons. The greater the emotional bond between persons, the more likely they will experience telepathy naturally. You've probably had experiences where you've thought the same thought, even the same words, almost simultaneously with another person.

▪ *Clairvoyance* is "clear-seeing." It involves images and visions of distant or inaccessible people, places, and objects with both inner and outer sight. Information or knowledge may arise spontaneously with the visions. Clairvoyance is a term that is being replaced by more modern ones, such as "medical intuition" to describe the ability to see into the body and its energy field to detect imbalances and disease, and "remote viewing" to describe seeing things at a distance.

▪ *Clairaudience* is "clear hearing." You hear information through an inner voice or through a "direct voice," which seems to originate in the space around you as though an invisible person were speaking to you.

Claire was getting ready to leave for the store when she heard a distinct inner voice say, "Don't go to the store." She immediately thought that this was silly, that there was no reason for her not to go. But strangely, she felt compelled to follow the directive, and so she postponed her plans. She later heard on the news that a gas main had exploded in front of the store at about the time she would have been there. Dozens of people were seriously injured.

Clairaudience also involves other sounds, such as music.

- *Clairsentience* is "clear sensing." It usually describes a range of physical sensations that convey information, such as smells, tastes, tactile perceptions, and bodily reactions (tightness in the belly, tingling of the skin, and so on). For example, your intuition tells you something is wrong when you experience a certain heaviness in your abdomen.

- *Psychokinesis (PK)* is the influence of mind over matter. Parapsychological research has established that we can alter the physical environment with our thought or will. In studies, subjects have altered the toss of dice, changed temperatures in rooms, and changed the properties of water, among other experiments. Healing at a distance is a form of PK, as is the weather control performed by shamans.

The Auric Field

You will understand your own intuition, and be able to develop it more quickly, with an understanding of your auric field— your energy blueprint. The aura is an envelope of vital energy that radiates from everything in nature: minerals, plants, animals, and humans. The aura is not perceivable by normal vision, but can be "seen" through the intuitive/psychic senses. It may be seen as a multicolored mist that fades off into space with no definite boundary, containing sparks, rays, and streamers. Or it may be felt as a textured substance, or even experienced as a collection of emotions or smells.

The existence of the aura has been known since ancient times—it appeared in the writings and art of Egypt, India, Greece, and Rome, among other civilizations. In the sixteenth century, Paracelsus was one of the first Western scholars to expound upon the astral body, which he described as a "fiery globe." In the eighteenth century, the clairvoyant Emanuel Swedenborg wrote in his *Spiritual Diary* that "there is a spiritual sphere surrounding every one, as well as a natural and corporal one." Scientific study of the aura began in the late eighteenth century, when Franz Anton Mesmer put forth the theory of "animal magnetism," an electromagnetic force that could be transmitted from one person to another and effect healing. In 1845, Baron Karl von Reichenbach, a German chemist, announced the discovery of the "odic force" energy. Reichenbach's clairvoyant test subjects sat in darkened rooms and saw flamelike energy radiating from fingertips, animals, plants, magnets, and certain crystals. The subjects described seeing flames of red, orange, green, and violet, which alternately appeared and disappeared; a violet red, which disappeared in a smokelike vapor; and intermingled sparks and stars among all colors.

Shortly before World War I, Dr. Walter J. Kilner, who was in charge of electrotherapy at St. Thomas's Hospital in London, discovered that the human aura could be made visible if viewed through an apparatus containing a coal-tar dye called dicyanin, which made ultraviolet light visible. Kilner saw the aura as a faint haze that sometimes could be separated into two or three portions. It enveloped the whole body.

While scientific measurement of the aura is still elusive, anyone who trains to become an energy healer knows the aura exists and learns how to perceive it and work with it.

From my own experience, I know that the aura exists. In the early 1980s, I began studying energy healing, learning a variety of techniques. The basic principle behind energy healing is that the healer is a channel for the universal life force, which has the power to heal. The universal life force is a substance that permeates everything in existence and is essential to life and health. It is known by various names, including chi, ki, prana, and mana. When we are full of the universal life force, we are healthy and vital. If we lack in it, we become ill. Healers channel the universal life force to others through their hands. They learn how to direct the life force through their perceptions of the auric field. Healers use their intuitive/psychic sense to perceive problem areas in the body and aura. According to energy medicine, problems occur first in the aura and then affect the body.

In energy healing, I learned how to feel and see the aura, and receive impressions related to another person's well-being. Energy work involves directing the universal life force to areas where it is lacking and thus is needed. I also learned how to clear and smooth blockages in the aura, which invariably resulted in an easing of physical symptoms.

The aura has several envelopes, or layers, to it. Various names are applied to them. Some esoteric traditions split the aura into as many as five or seven bodies. I see four primary bodies, or layers, which are most relevant to developing the intuition:

The etheric body. Immediately next to the physical body is the etheric body, which is an energy double of the physical. Many energy healers work in the etheric body, where they see symptoms of illness not yet manifested physically.

The emotional body. Next to the etheric body is the emotional body. This is the part of our energy field that retains impressions from our emotions. Many sources of illness can be detected here. Longtime emotional imbalances contribute to physical illness. As an energy healer, this is the body I naturally am attracted to when I look at someone's aura. I "see" such things as emotional wounds, repressed emotions, and emotional difficulties. These impressions are conveyed to me in images (many of which are symbolic and need to be intuitively interpreted), in words that arise inside my mind, and in the holistic, intuitive sense of "knowing."

The mental body. Next to the emotional body is the mental body, the plane of thoughts. In all mystical and esoteric traditions, thought creates reality. We become what we think. First we think it, then we say and do it. If you think you're a failure, you will create a reality of failure around you. If you think you're a success, you will create that reality instead. All of us deal with certain "programming" from our upbringing and conditioning that we must deal with in life. Negative programming needs to be altered if we are to achieve our fullest potential. All of us have the ability to change in significant ways—if we make the choice to do so and act on that choice.

The astral body. After the mental body comes the astral body. This outer layer extends off into space. It concerns our spiritual side—the soul part of us that is evolving through life. The Higher Self resides in this outer layer.

Intuitive impressions of the aura are subjective. Each person sees or feels the aura according to his or her own intuitive voice. Later on in this book, you will learn how to intuitively "read" an aura and how to move energy through your own auric field.

CHAKRAS

The universal life force enters the aura and body through centers called chakras, a Sanskrit term meaning "wheels." The chakras act as transformers, taking the universal life force and distributing it throughout the aura and body.

Chakras are called wheels because they are shaped like multicolored lotus petals or spoked wheels that rotate at various speeds as they process the universal life force. If the chakras are sluggish or blocked in movement, health is affected.

There are seven major chakras and hundreds of minor ones. The seven major chakras, which are most directly concerned with physical health, lie along the spinal column and the head, from the base of the spine to the top of the head. Each chakra is associated with a major endocrine gland, a major nerve plexus, a physiological function, and a psychic function. Each chakra also has its own unique number of spokes in its wheel. The higher the position along the spinal column, the more complex the chakra, the greater its number of spokes, and the higher its functions.

Each chakra has its own color associated with it. When the chakras are balanced and healthy, their colors are clear and luminous, and their rotation is smooth. In poor health, they become cloudy and irregular or sluggish in rotation. Chakras that are blocked are believed to adversely influence the body functions they govern. In alternative healing, there are techniques for clearing chakra blockages and stimulating rotation.

The seven major chakras are:

The root, located at the base of the spine. It is concerned with self-preservation; one's connection to family, country, and race; one's connection to the physical world; one's animal nature; and taste and smell. It is red in color.

The spleen, which lies near the genitals. It governs sexuality and reproduction; personal power; and ambition. It is orange-red.

The solar plexus, which rests just above the navel. It is associated with the emotions, gut instinct, and intuition. It affects the adrenals, pancreas, liver, and stomach. It is yellow.

The heart, which is located midway between the shoulder blades in the center of the chest. It governs the thymus gland and influences immunity to disease. It is linked to higher consciousness and unconditional love. It is green.

The throat, located at the base of the neck. It is associated with creativity and self-expression, and the search for truth. It also influences the thyroid and parathyroid glands, and metabolism, and is associated with certain states of expanded consciousness. It is silvery blue.

The brow, located on the forehead, above the nose. It is called the third eye for its influence over spiritual enlightenment. It is associated with the pituitary gland, the pineal gland, intelligence, intuition, and psychic powers. It is indigo.

The crown, located just above the top of the head. It is not associated with any glands, but reveals the individual's level of conscious evolution. It cannot be activated until all the other chakras are refined and balanced; when it is, it brings supreme enlightenment and cosmic consciousness. It is violet.

In the Key exercises in Part II, you will learn more how to work with the chakras to activate your intuitive faculty.

KUNDALINI AND INTUITION

The chakras are home to a psycho-spiritual energy, called kundalini. "Kundalini" is Sanskrit for "she who is coiled," named for the divine female creative energy, which lies coiled like a serpent in the root chakra. Kundalini slumbers away within us until it is activated by spiritual awakening or creativity. Developing the intuition also awakens kundalini, which opens higher powers within us.

The phenomena associated with it vary, and include strange physical sensations and movements, pain, clairaudience, visions, brilliant lights, superlucidity, psychical powers, ecstasy, bliss, and transcendence of self. Kundalini has been described as liquid fire and liquid light that pours through the body. A common experience of kundalini is a sensation of heat or tingling that begins at the base of the spine and travels up the body.

Kundalini experiences have been described in spiritual traditions around the world since ancient times. It is a universal phenomenon. When we awaken our higher centers of consciousness, we are filled with a new energy that brings heightened creativity and intuition.

Sometimes intuition is accompanied by sensations of heat, tingling, electricity coursing through the body, and buzzing or ringing in the ears. These phenomena also are linked to kundalini.

Chapter Three

Intuition Speak

THE INTUITION HAS FOUR PRIMARY AVENUES FOR CONVEY-
ing information to us:

- Body

- Mind

- Emotions

- Spirit

The Body

Intuition can make use of all of your physical senses to register itself for attention. The most common of these sensory experiences are:

PHYSICAL FEELINGS IN THE BODY

Strong body sensations are the most frequently reported type of "intuition speak." Examples are a tingling of skin, warmth, coldness, a peculiar sensation in the gut, tickling, and so on. Beethoven said his whole body shivered and his hair stood on end when inspiration struck. He felt plunged into a mysterious state of oneness with the world in which all the forces of nature were his instruments.

Most of the time our physical intuition cues aren't an intense mystical experience. But they do help to steer us in making decisions.

Jennifer was interviewing candidates for a job. She needed someone who could hit the deck running and would be reliable for meeting the tight deadlines coming up. The opening had drawn a large number of applicants, many of whom looked promising. Jennifer had interviewed many persons when she received an application from a woman whose resume looked great. She had all of the qualifications and more for the job. She had good references. What's more, her background made her an ideal addition to the company for the long-term picture. Jennifer scheduled an appointment for an interview and looked forward to meeting her. Maybe her search would come to an end.

When the woman walked into her office, Jennifer had an immediate, visceral reaction to her: she felt as though she had been punched in the abdomen. It was strong and took her by surprise. At first she thought she was having a reaction to something she'd eaten for lunch. Then she realized that it was more like an anxiety kind of feeling. She strove to disregard it and carry on with the interview.

The applicant was pleasant and eager for the job. She gave the rights answers to all of Jennifer's questions. She could start right away. The feeling in Jennifer's abdomen spread throughout her like a malaise. She began to feel as though she were in two separate worlds: talking to the job applicant and trying to analyze her own unease.

Jennifer thanked the woman and said she would be in touch.

Jennifer was puzzled. Why had she reacted so strongly to the woman? She reviewed the application. Everything looked terrific on paper. The interview itself had gone well. The next step would be to check the references and previous employment. But whenever Jennifer thought about hiring the woman, she felt a tightening in her gut. It seemed like a warning. Something wasn't right.

Jennifer decided not to pursue hiring the woman. She continued her search and found another candidate whose stated qualifications were good, though not as good as the woman's. When Jennifer interviewed that candidate, she experienced a warm, bouyant feeling, and a lightness in her abdomen. Everything professional checked out, and the person was hired.

Much later, Jennifer happened to learn that the woman who had seemed like the ideal candidate was in fact much the opposite. She had a history of troubles on the job. The information had validated Jennifer's gut-level warning. The person who was hired, meanwhile, performed better than might have been expected.

Jennifer experienced intuition speaking through strong body sensations. Her gut instinct gave her information not available to the rational mind.

VISIONS

The sense of sight can give us the big picture and the clear picture from our intuition. Pictures are powerful conveyors of information, much better than words. Most often, visual images play out on the inner eye. For example, you're struggling to come up with attractive packaging for a new product. Design after design goes in the waste bin. Suddenly, you get a flash of what the packaging should look like, seeing it very clearly. Or, you may get a picture of what may happen in the future—for example, the chart of a stock that you are interested in buying.

Sometimes images need to be interpreted. For example, I receive visual impressions when I do readings for others. Some images are straightforward, others are not. In one case, I saw a tennis ball bouncing back and forth across a net on a court. The image related to a situation in the client's life in which she was caught in the middle of a family dispute and felt bounced back and forth by the opposing sides.

In another case, I saw a piece of cauliflower over a man's throat chakra. I said to myself, "What does cauliflower have to do with the throat chakra?" A soon as I asked myself the question, the answer arose spontaneously within. In the blink of an eye, I understood that the man's self-expression was rather like a piece of cauliflower—bland and without definite form. He confirmed that he indeed was struggling with expressing himself in a bolder and more assertive way.

The images that your intuition delivers to you will always be appropriate for your own unique Intuition Speak.

The intuition also uses images to represent yes or no, such as a green light and a red light. These images may arise spontaneously, or we can train the intuition to use certain key images and symbols.

SOUNDS AND VOICES

Perhaps you hear a ringing or buzzing in the ears, or voices. "Whenever my intuition gives me a positive sign, I always hear bells ringing," a man told me at one of my workshops. "They sound like cathedral bells rung in celebration. Sometimes the sound is so distinct that I think there are bells somewhere actually ringing." A woman said she, too, heard sounds she associated with her intuition, chiefly rushing water that sounded like a huge waterfall.

It's not uncommon to hear voices say such things to you as "yes," "no," "forget it," "you have it," "don't worry," or offer specific instructions or advice: "Take the next train." Such voices usually seem to come from within and can be quite commanding.

Voices may also seem to emanate from the space around us. Throughout history, such voices have often been attributed to otherworldly sources, such as angels, spirit guides, the dead, saints, and even God. In ancient times, one could not earn a badge as a prophet unless one had audition experiences that evidenced direct communication with the divine.

Hearing voices is a phenomenon called "audition." Audition usually occurs in waking consciousness, or in meditative, contemplative, or distracted states of consciousness that are on the borders of sleep. Audition also occurs in dreams.

Paula, a teacher, told me, "When I ask my intuition for guidance, I often get an answer in a clear voice that seems to come from just above my shoulders. At first I thought it was a person speaking. Then I thought I was imagining things. But I have learned that the voice is invariably right, so I pay attention. It usually happens when I'm not concentrating about whatever I'm seeking guidance on."

TASTES

Yes, the intuition can use our taste buds to prod us in the right direction. Good tastes, bad tastes, dry mouth, stinging mouth, moist mouth all can be signals of yes or no. Some people experience particular tastes that are associated with personal pleasant or unpleasant situations. "When something isn't right, but not in an obvious sort of way, I'll often get a taste of iron in my mouth," a workshop participant said. "I don't know where it comes from. But I've learned over time that it happens whenever I should be careful, that something isn't as good as it seems to be."

SYNESTHESIA

Some people experience their intuition in an odd blending of senses, such as hearing colors or tasting shapes. This blending of senses is called "synesthesia," which comes from the Greek terms that mean "feeling together." A minority of the population experiences synesthesia as their norm all the time. Most synesthetes, as they are called, experience only one or two "crossed" connections; not all five senses are blended. The most common is colored hearing, in which certain sounds produce lines, spheres, or other simple geometric, colored shapes that appear in the person's near field of vision.

Although few people have synesthesia, researchers have hypothesized that the capability for it may have been part of our ancient and original blueprint. It may be closely allied to our so-called primitive instincts, which makes it a potential first cousin to the intuition. In the future, the ability to experience blended senses may be more the norm than the exception.

EXERCISE FOR THE SENSES

Everyone processes information through their senses in a different way. Typically, we have a dominant sense that registers the strongest impressions. Try this exercise to find out more about how your senses give you information:

Close your eyes, breathe deeply, and relax. Clear your mind of its busy thoughts. With each breath, feel yourself loosening and expanding.

Now imagine that you are in a beautiful forest, walking along a path. Look up at the trees . . . notice how green they are . . . the shapes of their trunks, branches and leaves. . . . Look at the brush and flowers alongside the path. . . . Notice the kinds of blossoms and the colors. . . . See the sky painted across the background. . . .

Feel the firmness of the path beneath your feet . . . the indentations in the ground . . . stones and pebbles. . . . Stop and touch a group of

flowers . . . feel the texture of the stems, the velvet of the blossoms. . . .
Touch the trees and feel their leaves. . . .

A breeze blows gently . . . it brings strange smells . . . identify the
smells . . . hear the breeze in the trees. . . .

Insects buzz in the air . . . small creatures rustle in the leaves . . .
your feet make soft noises on the path. . . . Still yourself and listen
for more subtle sounds. . . .

You come to a house . . . a picnic table has been set up outside the
house . . . on it is a freshly baked cherry pie. . . . You sit down and
eat a piece of pie and drink a beverage. . . . You savor each bite and
swallow. . . .

When you are finished eating, return your consciousness to the room.
Breathe deeply, pushing the breath down through the soles of your
feet. Open your eyes.

Make notes about your sensory experience. Which sense was strongest and most vivid for you? Perhaps you had two senses that were equally vivid. These are the senses most likely to convey intuitive impressions to you.

Emotions

Bodily sensations related to the intuition may be commonplace, but for many of us, the intuition speaks loudest through the emotions: good feelings, bad feelings, sad feelings, joy, elation, depression, dread—the entire range of human emotional expression.

Most of us have had at least one experience of intuition that manifested as inexplicable dread: we were about to do or undertake something, and an inexplicable dread took hold of us so that we changed our minds and actions accordingly.

Inexplicable and strong feelings also prompt us to do things that defy reason, but which are right. Mona Lisa Schulz, a psychiatrist, neuroscientist, and medical intuitive, describes many of these kinds of experiences in her book *Awakening Intuition: Using Your Mind-Body Network for Insight and Healing*. Once, on one of the first nights that Schulz was on duty as an intern in a hospital emergency room, an elderly woman was brought in after collapsing at home. She seemed to have recovered, but was admitted to stay overnight because no one was at home to care for her. Although nothing seemed to be obviously wrong with the woman, Schulz experienced something that told her otherwise:

> As I approached her gurney, I began to get a vague, fuzzy, yet insistent feeling that seemed to cut through all the noise and commotion around me. I just had a sudden conviction, seeming to come out of nowhere, that contrary to the physical evidence, all was not right with this patient.
>
> I wanted her to get an EKG. Don't ask me why. Her chart indicated no past history of heart trouble, and the examining physician hadn't noted any signs of cardiac problems.[1]

Schulz was able to prevail in getting an EKG ordered. Her intuition next directed her to check medical records. There, she found files on the patient documenting a history of heart problems. The EKG showed that she was not fine, but was having a heart attack. Schultz said her own gut instinct had helped to save the woman's life.

Because of it's link to emotions, intuition has long had the stereotype of being a "woman's thing." A woman's intuition typically is described in emotional terms as feelings—something women have and men don't admit to having. (Men are supposedly more "rational" and "logical.") The debate over the merit of emotion versus reason has been going on since ancient times. Plato viewed emotions as a prison and reason as the liberation from that prison. Aristotle countered that emotions have a logic of their own and have to be understood on their own terms. Our scientific worldview has favored Plato: reason is a "higher" function than emotion, and "knowledge" is based on what can be measured and quantified, not felt or experienced. Fortunately, those stereotypes are disappearing as we learn more about how intuition functions, how it works in conjunction with reason, and how both sexes use intuition as part of the human arsenal for innovation, success, and even survival in the world.

We are emotional as well as rational beings. The intuition speaks *through* emotions and is best able to guide us when we apply all of our thinking and feeling processes.

Emotional intuition brings great ideas and inspiration as well as direction. Feeling profoundly connected to nature or swept up in a tidal wave of emotion can literally flood us with intuitive light. Asked how he got his ideas for his compositions, Beethoven said many of them came out of his emotions. "They come to me in the silence of the night or in the early morning, stirred into being by moods," he said.[2]

The Mind

Intuition works on a mental level when we have sudden flashes of insight in which we see solutions to problems and information organized in new ways. Our creativity is fueled; we become visionaries of the future. Mental intuition results from brainstorming, concentration, and problem-solving efforts. Typically, we do an intense amount of left-brain thinking and analysis prior to the intuitive hit.

INSPIRATION

Inspiration—those experiences in which profound insights, information, intuitions, and creativity burst through in crystal clarity—is a form of intuition. Inspiration is behind all great leaps of creativity, genius, innovation, and invention. It's the proverbial bolt from the blue that enables us to see something in an entirely new light or see the big picture or see the future very clearly. Though very mental in nature, it may be accompanied by physical sensations such as chills, burning, tingling, "electric glows," and "fuzzy" feelings that something profound is about to happen.

We all experience inspiration, but, like other forms of intuition, it seems to naturally strike more often a gifted few. You needn't feel left out of the club. Developing your intuition will increase the flow of inspiration in all areas of your life. Your intuition makes you more aware of inspiration—and also shows you how to use inspiration.

Mental concentration must be balanced with relaxation. This prevents mental burnout, of course, but also is necessary in order for the inspiration to come through. Great artists and thinkers throughout history have known this. Mozart experienced inspiration during times when he was alone and in "good cheer," such as walking after a good meal or traveling in a carriage. The ideas flowed best and most abundantly, he said, and he heard his compositions all at once and not as successive parts. The music poured into his thoughts in finished form, needing only to be committed to paper. Inspiration struck hotel entrepreneur Conrad Hilton when he doodled. Einstein went sailing or canoeing to disengage his mind. His breakthrough to the Theory of Relativity came with what he called "the happiest thought of my life," when he was inspired by a daydream vision of a person falling off a roof. He realized that the person was both at rest and in motion simultaneously.

When we're trying to solve a problem or come up with new ideas, we can think and think and think about it and still wind up empty-handed (or empty-headed, as the case may be). We can think too hard, in fact. But if we set the matter aside, the answer is likely to burst forth on us when we are doing something entirely different, such as a pleasurable activity, routine tasks, or even while driving a car.

When we're in a state of passive receptivity, we're likely to be in an alpha state of consciousness. The brain waves move from the beta range (active thought and waking consciousness) to the alpha range when we meditate, pray, relax, and doze off. Many inspirations also strike in the borderlands of sleep. In the alpha state, our intuitive consciousness has freer range to roam and to make an impact on us. It doesn't have to compete with active thought. Ex-Beatle Paul McCartney once related that he woke up from sleep with the song "Yesterday" in his head. The poet William Wordsworth often awakened with poetry forming in his mind.

People who engage in aerobic activity, such as jogging, also experience an increase in inspiration. Aerobic activity has been shown to release a flood of endorphins and chemicals in the brain. This in turn stimulates right-brain kinds of experiences, even of a profound spiritual and mystical nature.

Some of my best ideas come when I am doing my daily workout on a stationary exercise bicycle. During my warm-up phase, I like to read something of a spiritual nature. My favorites are inspirational magazines such as *Science of Mind* and *Guideposts* because their articles are short and easy to read, yet full of good information. Reading them often sparks a tremendous flow of creative energy, so that by the time I am into the harder phase of the workout, I am no longer reading but deep into a stream of inspiration.

When I'm done, I write it all down while it's fresh and full of maximum energy. Inspirations are like dreams—you must record them, or you will lose their content.

I also find that inspirations often occur to me while I am gardening, an activity that gives me a great deal of pleasure, and when I am listening to pleasant music.

Spirit

Our intuition reaches beyond waking consciousness into the mysterious realms of spirit. Guidance may be given through spiritual experiences, dreams, and in the form of synchronicity.

SPIRITUAL CUES

My good friend Reverend Toni G. Boehm, founder of Awakening Hearts Ministry, calls intuition our "spiritual cues" from God. "Intuition is not just the ability to see the future, but more importantly is the ability to recognize the signals that we are being given in the moment that tell us that we are to do something different," Toni explained to me. "For example, we hear cues like turn left, leave now, call Sue immediately, don't take that job regardless of how lucrative it seems—the messages are infinite in nature.

"When we listen, when we go in a direction we don't understand but feel is right, one of two things—or both—are happening," Toni continued. "One is that something in us is ready to be healed, and the experience for the healing lies in the direction in which we are being led. The other is that someone else is ready to be healed and, on an unconscious soul level, we have said yes to participating as a catalyst or a participant in the healing."

DIVINE HELP

Like Toni, many people see the intuition as a form of guidance from higher powers. The intuitive voice or prompting comes from God, Goddess, spirit guides, angels, saints, Jesus, Mary, and other holy figures. The helpful intercession of spiritual beings provides a sense of personal comfort and support—we are secure in the knowledge that greater forces are watching out on our behalf. We feel closer to the Divine, the Great Mystery, because of this personal connection.

The certainty that the guidance comes from, say, angels, may begin with childhood experiences, or develop in the course of spiritual study or after a person has a mystical experience. The source of the guidance is identified by the intuition itself. We "know" the messenger and source of our guidance. The knowing arises spontaneously within us. It is our personal badge of Truth.

Patricia, a devout woman who prays and studies the Bible, identifies the sources of her guidance as Jesus and her guardian angel, who communicate through inner feelings and clear voices:

> One night several years ago, I was in my bed at home in a house with my brother and his wife. . . . I felt led by the Word—an inner feeling that I believe is Jesus Christ—telling me to pray that there would be angels around the swimming pool outside. We have a small above-ground pool in the backyard. There are a lot of children in the neighborhood, including my niece and nephew, who go into the pool. So, I prayed as directed. I envisioned angels standing around the pool's ledge facing inward. They looked like Roman guards, ready for protection. I don't know why they had that appearance, that's just how they popped up. I didn't anticipate that there might be an accident. In fact, I kind of questioned why I had been directed to pray that.
>
> A day or two later, I found myself in the pool with the little children. I don't know why I got in—I usually don't use it. Mostly, it's for the kids. They splash around with floaters on their arms to keep them up. I was standing in the water at one edge, and a friend came over and started talking to me, diverting my attention.
>
> My sister was nearby but out of sight. She suddenly felt the Lord say to her, "Check on Lisa," her daughter who is two-and-a-half years old. She looked around and realized Lisa

was not present. "Patty, is Lisa in the pool?" she called out. I didn't hear her, and she called out again, "Patty, is Lisa in the pool?" I heard her and turned around just in time to see my little niece step off the ladder into the pool at the other end without her little floaters on. She sank immediately under water. "Oh, my God!" I shouted, and I started running toward her in the water. But the water was heavy, and it seemed like I couldn't get to her in time. Then I heard an authoritative masculine voice, about a foot away from my right ear, say, "Swim to her!" I felt a presence, as though someone were standing near to me.

I swam to Lisa, and I scooped her out of the water by her arms. Her eyes were open so wide they almost seemed to pop out of her head. By then my sister had reached the pool, and she took Lisa and began banging her on the back. Water spurted out of her mouth, and she coughed and began breathing again. She was all right!

I thank the Lord that her life was saved. Lisa didn't suffer any damage. Truly, it was a miracle.

Later, I asked the Lord whose voice I'd heard in the pool, that said, "Swim to her!" It wasn't the voice of Jesus, because I know that voice. The answer was given to me that it was an angel. And I know it was.[3]

Psychotherapist and popular author Wayne W. Dyer recounts intuitive help that came as the voice of God:

On a vacation trip to Panama City, Florida, my wife was driving the car while my daughter Tracy and her cousin were asleep in the backseat. I was napping after six hours of driving. Suddenly an overwhelming insistence made me sit up, and I could see that the car in front of us was about to have a head-on collision with the car in front of it. My wife could not see over the car ahead of us and was unaware of what we

were heading for when the car in front of ours swerved toward the gravel alongside the road to avoid the collision. At
the same instant that the car swerved, I grabbed the wheel of
our car and moved us onto the gravel and the errant driver
suddenly became alert. Another horrible head-on crash was
avoided.

What was that intuitive feeling that righted me in that
instant? You call it what you want; I know it as God speaking to me.[4]

KNOWING TRUTH

The highest function of intuition transcends the physical
realm and literally brings us a holistic understanding of the universe. In mysticism, intuition is the means by which to achieve
direct and immediate Truth and knowledge of the most intimate
secrets of life. The discovery of Truth is a unique spiritual journey
for every person. The great Indian mystic Sri Aurobindo described
intuition as "a memory of the Truth." You do not discover something unknown through intuition, but rather discover yourself.

You need not be a yogi or ascetic to have an experience of
mystical intuition. A practice of deep meditation or contemplation can bring intuitive flashes that reveal the ineffable nature of
the cosmos, the Divine Force, the soul and the unity of all things.
P. D. Ouspensky gave the name "Tertium Organum" to what he
called "intuitive logic" or "higher logic," defined as the "logic of
infinity, the logic of ecstasy," which he said has existed since time
immemorial in great philosophical systems and holds the key to
the Mysteries. The formula of this intuitive logic may be expressed
as "A is both A and not A," or "A is All." Ouspensky said Plotinus'
treatise, *On Intelligible Beauty*, embodies the fullest expression of
this logic. Plotinus said that "every thing contains all things in
itself . . . so that all things are everywhere, and all is all. . . . And
the splendour there is infinite."[5]

DREAMS

Dreams have been used since antiquity for guidance and problem-solving. Our ancestors the world over regarded dreams as a direct line of communication to the gods. Dreams were revered as divine gifts; through them, the gods dispensed wisdom, prophecy, and direction.

Historically, the understanding of dreams was the province of specially trained priests or dream professionals. These dream wizards could help others interpret their dreams. They also used dreams to pose questions to the gods. Incubation rituals focused intent upon a question; the answer was expected to be revealed during sleep. The Greeks and Romans especially used dreams for healing. Ailing people would make pilgrimages to special dream temples, where they would incubate dreams for healing. They hoped to be healed in their dreams, or to be given prescriptive information that would aid their healing.

The same truth about the power of dreams still applies today. Dreams tap into the intuitive resources of our Higher Self. They also deliver messages of spiritual import to us. Our dreams are a hot line to the Creator. We often talk about the need to "sleep on it" before rendering a final decision. In sleep, our intuition helps us sort through information to arrive at a clear answer. The answer may appear in dreams, or may become clear upon awakening. Today we know that everyone, not just the specially trained, can work effectively with his or her dreams.

I have been interested in dreams for most of my life. I consider them one of my greatest intuition allies. My dreams are a constant source of intuitive guidance and creative inspiration. The more I pay attention to them, the more responsive they are.

Sometimes we discover the intuitive power of dreams inadvertently. Jan was offered a job in another city. It was an attractive offer in money, responsibility and opportunity. Yet Jan wasn't sure she wanted to uproot herself and move. She argued back and forth with herself, listing pros and cons, unable to arrive at a decision that felt right. She had a limited period of time in which to give an answer to her prospective employer.

After wrestling with it unsuccessfully, Jan said to herself, "I can't think about it anymore tonight. I'll worry about it in the morning."

That night, she had a dream in which she was in a sailboat obscured by fog. She couldn't see where she was going.

"When I woke up, I knew what my decision was," Jan told me. "I knew the job wasn't right for me."

I asked her how she knew that the dream reflected her right choice and not just her state of uncertainty.

"It was the feeling I had when I awakened," she said. I just *knew* that if I took the job and moved, I would feel kind of lost."

The imagery of the sailboat was appropriate for Jan, who is an avid sailor.

Chris is a man who works in finance. For years, he has steeped himself in the business of investments and money decisions. He didn't pay much attention to his dreams until he had one about a stock. In his dream, he saw the price of the stock very clearly. It was much lower than it had been selling for. A couple of weeks later, an unexpected turn of events for the company adversely affected the price of the stock to the amount shown in his dream.

Intrigued, Chris then began asking his dreams for guidance about investments: when to buy, when to sell. A few times he followed his dream intuition even when it ran counter to what he knew by fact and analysis. "I've done very well with my personal portfolio," he said. "Would I have made the same decisions without the dream guidance? Some of them probably not."

Dreamwork may seem daunting at first because the imagery in dreams seems strange or bizarre. Taken literally, dreams don't seem to make much sense. Our dreams speak to us in images that are symbols. Learning one's own dream language is surprisingly easy. Merely setting our intention to understand our dreams opens the door to understanding them.

Dream incubation is discussed in Key #12.

SYNCHRONICITY

Many times our intuition speaks to us not from within but from without. It's as though the external world, even the universe itself, organizes just for us. People make offhand remarks that give us the answer we seek. We "just happen" to meet someone who provides a solution, or "just happen" to see a book that tells us what we need to know. These so-called meaningful coincidences are called synchronicity. They are no accidents of nature. They are part of the ordering of intuition and a divine plan for wholeness and balance. When we are in need, we send out a call to the universe. Perhaps we do it consciously by asking for help and guidance; perhaps we do it unconsciously by floundering in a pool of confused thoughts and emotions, or simply by having a need to fulfill. We get an answer back that guides us toward wholeness. Sometimes the answer is presented through synchronicity. It may be the best way for us to receive the answer. It may be the best way to get our attention after we have failed to pay attention or follow the inner voice. And, it may be the best way to validate opportunities.

Synchronicity gives us the feeling of a greater force at work, as though our destiny and purpose were being played out as part of a grand cosmic tapestry. It's not just a feeling. It's the Truth.

After I met my husband, Tom, an amusing synchronicity began calling his attention to the import of our relationship:

> On our second date, we got in Tom's car, and the radio came on when he started the ignition. The station that was tuned in was playing an old Simon & Garfunkel hit, "Scarborough Fair." "There's that song again!" Tom exclaimed. He went on

to tell me that since meeting me, he was hearing the song everywhere—it was on the radio nearly every time he turned it on. Friends sang it for no apparent reason. He even caught himself singing it in the shower one morning. It kept running through his mind.

Now, "Scarborough Fair" is not one of those golden oldies that one hears with great frequency on the radio. But for us, it had importance because a refrain line mentions several herbs, including rosemary. The fact that Tom was hearing this song a lot meant one thing: synchronicity, or "meaningful coincidence." It was the universe speaking: pay attention! I had to laugh.[6]

In her work as an intuitive teacher and counselor, Carol Adrienne has witnessed numerous stories of the amazing impact of synchronicity as a form of intuitive guidance: career changes, moves, relationships, creativity, business decisions, and more. "I am convinced more than ever that each of us must be alert for the tiny intuitions and ideas that show us where we need to pay attention, and what we need to develop," Carol says in her book, *The Purpose of Your Life*. "Even when we feel blocked and stagnant—as I certainly have been many times—I believe that we are simply at one particular *stage* of the unfolding life purpose that we came to fulfill."[7]

Carol's own unfoldment as artist, author, numerologist, and intuitive teacher came through many synchronicities: unexpected meetings with people, unexpected phone calls, nudges from others, opportunities that suddenly jumped into focus. She was guided to move, guided to return to school, guided to pursue various career moves. She had the courage to follow her guidance even when the obstacles against her success seemed daunting.

"Synchronicities seem to be external answers to an internal psychic state," Carol said. "For example, perhaps we need some particular information and unexpectedly we run into someone who provides us with exactly what we needed. Synchronicities are a moment in time when we are united with people or information in a way that cannot be described by a linear explanation. They cause us to stop and think. Another name for them is Providence."[8]

It was through synchronistic providence that Carol became partners with James Redfield, author of the hugely popular novels *The Celestine Prophecy* and *The Tenth Insight: Holding the Vision. The Celestine Prophecy* (once the biggest-selling nonfiction book in the world), acquainted readers with the concept that everything that happens in our lives has a deeper meaning. Carol read the book at the urging of others ("Over the years, I have learned to listen when people tell me things, so I went out and bought the book," she said). She began to apply the lessons in the book to her counseling practice. One day, an inner prompting urged her to remark about the book to her agent. That led to her collaboration with Redfield to write the nonfiction guides to his novels, *The Celestine Prophecy: An Experiential Guide* and *The Tenth Insight: Holding the Vision: An Experiential Guide*. Both books were bestsellers and gave tremendous boosts to Carol's own work.

Some of our most important synchronicities come in the words of other people, as demonstrated in Carol's case. Carol calls it the "people have been telling me" syndrome. If others keep urging you to do or try something, you should pay attention, especially if the remarks are unexpected and come from a disparate range of persons. I have experienced this syndrome myself, in my own life, and in the lives of others.

"People are always telling me I should paint," said Gladys, a participant in one of my workshops. Gladys, however, did not feel she had much artistic talent. She thought that her little drawings and handmade notecards for friends and family did not rank as professional art. She thought that others were "trying to be nice" by urging her to paint professionally.

"Perhaps you should listen," I told her. "Think of it this way:

it's not so much your friends urging you to paint, but God speaking to you through your friends."

That made a lot of sense to Gladys, and she pledged that she would take action with lessons.

Months later, I received a phone call from a happy and excited Gladys. She had begun lessons with some fear and trepidation at being exposed as ordinary. But her teacher quickly saw her innate talent and helped her to develop it. Gladys surprised herself not only by excelling, but by being caught up in a flow of wonderful energy at her newfound confidence and artistic creativity. "I'm so glad I listened," she said. "It's the best thing that ever happened to me."

A few months later, I received an invitation to her first gallery exhibition.

The concept of synchronicity is not new, but has been recognized since ancient times. In Eastern philosophy, it is represented in the idea of Tao, or All, and being "in the flow" with the field of the Tao. When we are in the flow, we are in harmony with everything else, and all goes along well. Western philosophy evolved away from a holistic view toward dualism. Synchronicity does not fit into dualism because it runs contrary to traditional "laws" of cause and effect. Today we know from quantum physics that causality only partially explains the workings of the universe. Everything is interrelated without dependence upon time or space.

Carl G. Jung helped to restore the concept of synchronicity for the West. Interestingly, he was intuitively inspired by Albert Einstein. Jung and Einstein met several times between 1909 and 1913, when Einstein was a professor in Zurich. Einstein's work on his theory of relativity inspired Jung to ponder a possible relativity of time as well as space.

No insight emerged for Jung until a decade later. As he explored the nature of the collective unconscious, he encountered numerous synchronicities he could not explain and that defied the odds of chance by astronomical figures. For example, he noted two incidents that happened to the wife of a patient: upon the deaths of her mother and grandmother, birds gathered outside the windows of the death-chambers. Jung knew that in many mythologies, birds represent the soul and are messengers to the gods. That they would gather at the moment of death, when the soul is believed to ascend to heaven, and not at another random time, constituted synchronicity.

Jung found further inspiration for synchronicity from other sources: the *I Ching*, which was introduced to him by Richard Wilhelm, and the work of physicist Wolfgang Pauli, a Nobel Laureate and associate of Einstein who proved the existence of nonlocal causality. Jung and Pauli collaborated on writing *The Interpretation and Nature of the Psyche*, of which Jung's essay, "*Synchronicity*," forms the second part.

In addition, Jung considered the theory of seriality, developed by Paul Kammerer. According to Kammerer, there is a "principal in nature which acts selectively on form and function to bring similar configurations together in space and time; it correlates by affinity."[9]

Jung said synchronicity can be found in events that do not coincide in time and space as well as in events that do, and that have meaningful psychological connections. Synchronicity links the material world to the psychic realm—the world of paranormal phenomena—and the archetypal realm. In other words, synchronicity acts like a bridge between different worlds of awareness. It serves as a conduit for information to travel from the land of the gods to our waking consciousness.

Sometimes synchronicities must happen repeatedly to get our attention. Gregg Levoy, author of *Callings: Finding and Following an Authentic Life*, recounts a series of unusual synchronicities related to a change in his consciousness. After a coveted job as a journalist did not work out, Levoy felt depressed, lost, and embarrassed. One day he drove home from work listening to a song called "Desperado," sung by the Eagles. The lyrics refer to a queen of hearts. When he got out of his car, Levoy found a queen of hearts playing card lying on the curb. At the time, his spiritual path had not yet opened, and so Levoy filed the incident away as a curiosity.

For several years, Levoy searched for a sense of direction in his life. At various intervals, and always in improbable places, he would find a queen of hearts playing card. One even showed up on a sand dune in Oregon.

The meaning of the synchronicities eventually made itself clear to him:

> I came to understand this rather profound administering of chance as directing me toward something that both my writing and my life needed at that time: more heart, less head; more intuition, less intellect; more confessing, less preaching; more of the inner life, the emotional life, the life of the senses; more listening, more following, more of what Carl Jung referred to as the anima, the force of the feminine in a man's life. The queen, of course, is the *archetype* of femininity— of powerful femininity—and I felt myself being compelled toward this energy by the kind of meaningful coincidence that Jung called synchronicity.[10]

Awareness of synchronicity triggers more synchronicity. The more we believe that events have a spiritual purpose and are not random, the more we are aided by synchronicity.

The argument is made that synchronicity negates free will: that we are at the mercy of whatever tide we ride. I do not at all believe that to be the case. Matter constantly reorganizes itself according to affinities. Through free will—our thoughts, choices and actions—we change what is attracted to us. The more positive and assertive we are, the better we are able to achieve our goals. The more negative we are, the more we hold ourselves back and delay or prevent our success. And if we choose simply to ride the tide—the "whatever tide"—then that's what we get: "whatever." Synchronicity is a reflection of the results of your free will choices.

If you've been riding the "whatever tide," you can stop wasting time and energy now. Use your intuition to get on the track you want. Synchronicity will provide validation and course corrections.

It's All Interconnected

As you become better acquainted with your intuition, you will find that it has no sharply defined medium of communication with you. You may experience a predominance of one kind of medium or another, but most of your intuitions will overlap the categories described above. Intuition is not just a bodily phenomenon or strictly an emotional phenomenon, or a mental phenomenon or a spiritual one. The inner knowing is a combination of all of those things—you cannot separate one from the other.

Chapter Four

Opening Your Intuition Gate

INTUITION GIVES US THE ABILITY TO SEE AND UNDERSTAND our circumstances clearly. It enables us to cut through the murk of uncertainty and doubt. It clears obstructions in our path. Once you allow your intuition to function more freely, everything around you will snap into a different focus.

That doesn't mean, however, that you will be bombarded constantly by unwanted input. You will naturally learn how to open up and how to close down.

Use these guidelines to open your intuition gate. They will augment the skill-building exercise in Part II and the practical application exercises in Part III.

SET YOUR INTENTION TO BE INTUITIVE

The intention you set is simply acknowledging your intuitive ability. If you haven't felt intuitive in the past, it's because you have ignored or denied your innate ability. Successful people are not successful because they're convinced they're failures. They're successful because they see themselves that way.

Shifting your attitude about your intuition will open an amazing gate, and insights will come tumbling out.

At the start of every day, resolve that you will be intuitive, and that your intuition will serve you in all ways.

USE AFFIRMATIONS

One effective way to set your intention is through affirmations. Affirmations are positive statements that discipline the mind and help us to achieve that which we affirm. Through affirmations, we envision our goals as though we have already obtained them—an important change of consciousness for success.

Affirmations train the mind in positive thinking. They help us to let go of unproductive negative mind-sets that hinder us, such as "I never seem to know the right thing to do."

Affirmations are declarations that activate the Law of Mind. According to the philosophy of Science of Mind, founded by Ernest Holmes, we are surrounded by an Infinite Intelligence, or Mind (God), which functions upon our beliefs. If we let go of destructive beliefs and replace them with constructive ones, we enter into a cooperation with this Mind that enables us to be healthier, happier, more successful, and more spiritually fulfilled. To this end, daily affirmations—as well as meditation and prayer—facilitate that objective.

Holmes taught that there is but one Mind and everything is an aspect of It; each of us uses a portion of It. He taught, "My thought is in control of my experience, and I can direct my thinking," and "the ability to control my experiences and have them result in happiness, prosperity, and success lies in my own mind and my use of It."

"Mind responds to mind," said Holmes. "It is done to you as you believe." In other words, do not ask for things, but *declare* them. This is the Law of Mind, which manifests the beliefs we speak into It.[1]

Affirmations can be applied to any situation or need in life. *I have the perfect and right job for me* is an example of an affirmation that launches a search for a new job. *I enjoy perfect health* is an affirmation that helps us to maintain health as well as to heal.

Here are some affirmations for the intuition:

- *I am intuitive*

- *My intuition speaks clearly to me*

- *My intuition is always right*

- *I always know what to do*

- *I am always guided to make the right decisions*

- *I receive God's guidance through my intuition*

Some people feel that affirmations are more powerful when they insert their names into them: "I, Samantha Jones, am intuitive" or "I, Samantha, am intuitive." I have used affirmations with and without my name and find both styles effective. Use whichever style attracts you.

People sometimes tell me that affirmations don't work for them. They say they use them religiously, but nothing changes.

For affirmations to work, they must penetrate deeply into our consciousness. Many people say affirmations, but they allow them to only float on the surface of their minds, like boats floating on water. Affirmations are like deep probes. They must be sent below the surface into the core of our being. This is the center where conviction is born.

Affirmations work when they anchor deep within our consciousness, where they facilitate change. Affirmations alone do not make change. We must act on our affirmations. It's no good to recite affirmations throughout the day if our words, thoughts, and actions are the opposite. I've known more than a few people who talk affirmations for prosperity, but take no action to improve their finances and spend a lot of time complaining to others about their poverty.

We must *live* affirmations as well. If your affirmation is to be more financially prosperous, then you must live the affirmation. Do not complain to your friends about your lack and your debt. Making jokes about your debt or making self-effacing, self-critical remarks is counterproductive. Do not descend into envy because your neighbor bought a new car and you can't afford one.

You live the affirmation by doing whatever you can to bring it into manifestation. For financial prosperity, for example, you begin by giving thanks for all the things that you do have, for whatever resources you have. You give thanks for what you can afford. You save. You invest. You look for opportunities to prosper. You set goals and work toward them. You give thanks for your progress. You see the goals as fully realized, *now*.

Norman Vincent Peale, the godfather of the power of positive thinking, said that in order for positive thinking to work, we must believe in our goal in every cell of our being and picture it as already manifested. Holmes stressed this as well: we must believe with our total being.

When you say, "I am intuitive," you must believe it. You must act on it by paying attention and following your guidance.

There are five simple points to remember for success with affirmations:

1. *Create a clear affirmation*

2. *Believe in every cell of your being that it is right for you*

3. *See yourself as having achieved or attained your goal now*

4. *Ask for guidance and help through your intuition*

5. *Do everything you can to create your new reality*

Create—Believe—See—Ask—Do.

Make a commitment to work with affirmations on a daily basis. Create several. Every day, write them out fifteen times each. The repetition will focus your intent and set your intuitive consciousness to work on them full-time. Record your results. You will experience some changes immediately. Other changes may take longer. Be patient and persistent.

For more material on the practical applications of affirmations, see Chapter 14.

GIVE THANKS

Whenever we use affirmations, whenever our intuition comes through for us, it's important to give thanks. Thank your Higher Self, the Universe, God. Acknowledging blessings helps us to keep a balanced perspective on our connection to the Divine, and brings even greater blessings.

KEEP AN OPEN HEART

One facet of intuition is that it is the wisdom of the heart. It flourishes when we keep an open heart toward ourselves, others, and life. If you constantly think ill of others, if you are often suspicious of others, if you are always worrying that something dreadful—or the worst—is going to happen, you are closing your heart. The heart wisdom sees potential, not limit. It sees love, not anger or fear.

You can give yourself a quick heart intuition test anytime. Place your hand over your heart and ask, "From the depths of my heart, is this the right thing for me to do?" Do you feel heavy in the heart, or light? Your heart will give you the answer.

LEARN YOUR OWN INTUITION SPEAK

Everyone experiences intuition in unique ways. Study Chapter 3 on "Intuition Speak" and do a self-assessment. Even if you're a beginner in intuitive development, you will recognize some of the ways that your intuition communicates with you.

Do all of the exercises in Part II. They are designed to awaken and train the intuition in a wide variety of ways. They will reinforce the obvious ways your intuition communicates and develop the more subtle ways. The more you expand your intuitive awareness, the more information you will have to make the best decisions. You will recognize problems much earlier.

Don't be in a hurry to cover all the exercises quickly. Spend time learning them well so that you absorb them.

Pay attention also to your behavior. Take note of what happens to you when you are certain that something is right or wrong. Do you welcome intuition, or do you unconsciously shut it down by discounting it?

KEEP PRACTICING

The more you practice the exercises, the stronger your intuition will become. You will begin to use intuition more proactively than reactively.

LET GO OF ATTACHMENTS TO FEELINGS

One of our biggest distractions to intuition is emotion. Attachments to emotions, especially negative ones such as anger, fear, and guilt, prevent us from having access to intuition, which has no inherent emotion or bias. When strong feelings arise, try to detach yourself from them. Allow them to happen, then let go of them. Be receptive to new feelings that arise—they may surprise you.

Many emotional attachments belong to events or circumstances long past. By living more in the moment, you will be less likely to carry a lot of emotional attachment around with you.

DO YOUR HOMEWORK

Problems do not solve themselves. Genius does not strike the unprepared. The intuitive breakthrough is the extra measure that rewards those who work toward their goals. Great ideas, creativity, and solutions are achieved by examining situations from all possible angles, by applying one's rational knowledge and skill—and by being open to seeing situations in a new and different way.

Intuition expands upon a person's abilities, talents, and efforts. A symphony is not likely to fall into the head of someone who hasn't studied music. If you wish to apply your intuition to making investments, for example, then study the markets. Simple energy healing can be done without knowing much about the body, but if you wish to be a highly skilled medical intuitive, you must learn anatomy and physiology.

Whatever you seek to do in life, intuition can help you do it better.

James King Hill Jr., made headlines when he discovered a huge find of high-quality emeralds in Hiddenite, North Carolina. His success can be attributed to hard work and research, intuition and persistence. He just didn't go out into the hills one day on an inspiration.

As he explained to the media, treasure hunting was his first love from childhood. After trying various jobs, he knew he wanted to devote all of his time to hunting for gems.

His research told him that his best bet for a good find was Hiddenite, a tiny town about fifty miles from Charlotte in the Brushy Mountains. Small amounts of gems had been found there, but nobody considered it to be the site of exceptional treasure. Hill had some small strikes, but not the big one that he was convinced was there.

For thirty years, Hill held to his vision. He *knew* the treasure he sought was there. People said he was crazy. He ran out of money and went into debt. Just when things looked their darkest and it seemed like he might be forced to give up, a friend who also was inspired by vision put up the money to give him one more chance. This time, Hill hit pay dirt. The emeralds found were judged among the best in North America.

A research curator of geology made this observation about Hill: "He was very systematic and careful in learning what he needed to know. He found the emeralds he always thought were there."[2]

Fortunately, most of us don't have to persist thirty years to see an intuition fulfilled. But Hill's story serves as a good example of following intuition against the grain of opinion and experience. Hill did his homework, then followed his vision.

TRUST YOUR GUIDANCE

Your intuition is always right. People sometimes say to me, "Well, my intuition is usually right, but in this case it wasn't. . . ." Wrong. The intuition was right. It was over-ridden by imposed "shoulds," second-guessing, and desires. Sometimes we mistake zeal and enthusiasm for intuition. We act impulsively instead of intuitively. Or we are so desirous of a particular goal that we convince ourselves a particular course of action is right.

The intuition must be sought impartially. We cannot get clear guidance if we are wedded to a particular pursuit or idea.

Don't negate, rationalize, or judge your guidance. Examine it. If it conflicts with your projected desires, consider why.

When it comes to making a decision, your fence-sitting, doubts, uncertainty, ambivalence, and reservations may be the intuition's way of saying no. It's best not to proceed with a course of action unless you are clear that it is the right course.

If you feel stuck, ask a question and flip a coin. You will either feel elated or disappointed in the result. Upon closer examination, you'll see that your intuition was speaking to you all along.

Intuition can seem to go beyond logic. Go with it. Albert Einstein attributed some of his greatest ideas to a "free invention of the imagination" rather than to the brainpower of inductive logic. One morning as he arose from bed, Einstein saw in his mind's eye the image of a person riding on a beam of light. From that, he made his breakthrough insight into the relativity of time.

DON'T WORRY ABOUT BEING RIGHT

Naturally, we want to make decisions that are right. Sometimes we have a lot at risk. This puts a great deal of pressure on us to be right.

It may seem strange, but in order to be intuitive, you cannot be concerned with being right. Your very anxiety will interfere with the intuitive process. Fears, hopes, and expectations all have no place in intuition.

You must trust your guidance, and trust that whatever it is, it will be right.

Sometimes the right answer is not what we expect. If we cloud our minds and hearts with expectations, we may not hear the truth.

ACT ON YOUR GUIDANCE

Your intuition is not a complete process until you act on it. Taking action strengthens the intuitive faculty. It keeps a positive flow of energy circulating from divine supply through you to manifestation. If you ask the muse for help, you must honor the process in full.

Sometimes acting on guidance isn't easy, especially when we're not certain about where the guidance is taking us. You must trust your intuition.

Lynn felt she was in a dead end in her job. She had worked in the same field for more than twenty years and was bored. She felt she needed a change, but to what? She wasn't certain what else she wanted to do. Or even was qualified to do. The idea of retraining for new job skills was daunting. And, she was reluctant to change and risk losing job security and health benefits.

One morning Lynn awakened with these words ringing in her head: *Go back to school.* "It was clear as a bell and very commanding," she told me. "But I thought, why would I want to do that?"

In fact, the idea of going back to school was more intimidating than staying in her stale job. She was in her early fifties and could not envision herself on a campus with much younger students. Wasn't she too old to start over again? And even if she did go back to school, what would she study? How would she pay for it? She certainly couldn't afford to quit her job and go to school full-time.

Rational objections crowded her mind. Nonetheless, Lynn couldn't shake the idea. It seemed to pop up periodically as a reminder. For example, she would be in a conversation and learn about someone else deciding to go back to school. Or her attention would be caught by a prominent ad for a college. She randomly opened a women's magazine to a story about loans for second college educations.

Finally, Lynn began to think that perhaps school might be a good idea—but she still didn't know what she would study for another degree. One day she was watching television and a commercial flashed a big advertising slogan on the screen: "Just for fun."

Just for fun. Suddenly Lynn felt as though a brilliant burst of light went off inside her. Instead of making a commitment to a big plan of study, why not just take a course for the pure fun of it? The idea felt right.

When Lynn had been much younger and in leaner financial times, she had sewn many of her own clothes. She liked sewing and others had always complimented her on creations. She usually improvised on patterns. She had an eye for putting colors and textures together in novel ways. But with work, marriage, and home responsibilities, Lynn had given up sewing. In fact, she no longer even had a sewing machine.

"Wouldn't it be fun to take a class in interior decorating?" she thought.

Lynn found an adult education class in interior home design. She would need a sewing machine, but she didn't want to invest in a new one in case the class didn't work out. She found a good used sewing machine at a yard sale.

Lynn thoroughly enjoyed the class. She rekindled her interest in sewing. The talent that she'd displayed years ago and that she had dismissed as ordinary shined forth in a new light, impressing students and instructor alike. She felt totally absorbed in her art. When a student complimented her by saying, "You're a pro!" Lynn had another intuitive insight.

Lynn polished her skill, took some more courses, and began doing small jobs for others for nominal fees. She worked at home in the evenings and on weekends. She didn't advertise because she wanted only a small amount of work. Word of mouth, however, brought increasing business.

Her newfound second career gave her a recharge of energy and enthusiasm. Lynn decided not to give up her full-time job because of its steady income and benefits, and to thus limit her second career as a decorator to projects that she could manage in her available time. She found so much creative fulfillment in her decorating and sewing that her primay job no longer seemed so dull and oppressive.

She realized that her intuition had given her just the guidance she needed. It had come in a series of promptings. At first, she had seen her dilemma as all-or-nothing: a complete job/career change. She piled up the negatives. But the signals continued to move her in the right, though unexpected, direction.

ENJOY YOURSELF

Remember that mental concentration must be balanced by relaxation for the intuition to order information for a breakthrough insight. Nourish your intuition by taking time to play.

For inventor Nikola Tesla, relaxation often yielded a breakthrough. The inventor of alternating current motors and generators, the radio (wrongly credited to Marconi) and robotics, Tesla was steeped in knowledge about electrical technology. He was highly imaginative and developed many of his inventions in his imagination.

Tesla received his intuition for alternating current while he was out enjoying himself. He had designed a machine that had received the ridicule of one of his professors. He had not yet solved his problem of redesign when he went out one day with a friend. They walked through a park and recited poetry. Tesla was in a good mood and not thinking about his design problem when suddenly the solution hit him.

> The idea came like a flash of lightning and in an instant
> truth was revealed. I drew with a stick on the sand the dia-
> grams shown six years later in my address before the Ameri-
> can Institute of Electrical Engineers. . . . The images I saw
> were wonderfully sharp and clear and had the solidity of
> metal and stone, so much so that I told [my companion]:
> "See my motor here, watch me reverse it." I cannot begin to
> describe my emotions. Pygmalion seeing his statue come to
> life could not have been more deeply moved. . . . For a while
> I gave myself up entirely to the intense enjoyment of pictur-
> ing machines and devising new forms. It was a mental state
> of happiness about as complete as I have ever known in life.
> Ideas came in an uninterrupted stream and the only difficulty
> I had was to hold them fast. . . . I delighted in imagining the

motors constantly running, for in this way they presented to
the mind's eye a more fascinating sight. In less than two
months I evolved virtually all the types of motors and modi-
fications of the system which are now identified with my
name.[3]

Tesla did his homework by applying his knowledge and rational thought. His intuition vaulted him to a new level of insight. Note how his emotions validated his inspiration.

FOLLOW EVEN SMALL PROMPTINGS

One of the most amazing gifts the intuition brings us is a
strengthening of the bond among human hearts. We have more
empathy for others, which enables us to be more charitable, understanding, helpful, and forgiving. We are guided to do things
for others, especially acts of service and kindness that may seem
small to us but have a significant impact on the recipients. Thus,
we become better and better channels for the blessings of the
Creator to flow through us and out into the world.

Reverend Jayne Howard Feldman is an author and popular
speaker on angels. From childhood, she has felt a close relationship
to the angelic host, whose presence is the source of constant guidance. Many times Jayne finds herself prompted to do things that
do not make sense at the time. The purpose unfolds later. Because
she has learned to trust the guidance, Jayne follows it, knowing
that there is a good reason for it and that God is using her to help
others.

One day she browsed through a jewelry catalog and was attracted to a pair of simulated diamond earrings in the shape of
angels:

I heard my guardian angel tell me that I should buy these
earrings. I questioned that message, even though these were

truly precious, because I have a pair of diamond studs that my boyfriend, Walt, gave me for Christmas two years earlier, and I never take them out. I adore them! I could not fathom that I would ever wear these earrings in the catalog. However, I heard loud and clear that I was to buy them, and so I did.

The earrings arrived and sat in their little gift box on my dresser for about a month. Then one day I received a phone call from a close friend in New York. This wonderful woman had just returned from the doctor's office, where she had been told that she had cancer of the uterus. She was so frightened by the bleak prognosis. And she was very confused about decisions she had to make, and she knew she had to make them quickly. She asked if I would pray for her, and I told her I would begin immediately.

When I hung up the phone at my desk . . . and had got up from my chair, I felt myself encircled by the most loving angels of service, who were chiming to me in unison that I needed to go home at lunchtime and package up the earrings—they were for this woman to wear. They were to be sent to her immediately as a gift from the angels with this message: when she wore them, the angels would be there whispering in her ears, "We love you. It's going to be all right. Don't be frightened. We are here with you. You are not alone." The angels added that I was to tell this woman that she was to wear these earrings in "good health," because that was what the angels were sending her—blessings of good health. And so I followed those instructions and the earrings were on their way to New York.

Several days later, I received a call from my friend. She stated that the earrings had arrived on a day when she was having a battery of exams and tests, and they were truly a gift of strength from heaven. My friend commented that this had been one of the lowest days in her life until the angelic gift of love arrived. She felt the earrings were truly a miracle. She has since shared with me the inspiration that the earrings have given her to face the challenges at this time. The angels constantly reassure her by the presence of the "angelic present" that she is not alone and to open herself to the gifts of heaven, which include healing—and sometimes even a pair of earrings![4]

Jayne easily could have dismissed the prompting. Without an obvious reason, why buy the earrings? The rational mind could argue that it would be a waste of money. Note that an entire month elapsed before the purpose of the earrings became apparent in another intuitive prompting from the angels. Following inner guidance often requires patience, perseverance, and faith that the guidance is correct.

Jayne's story also demonstrates that following our guidance often means releasing attachment and expectation. Though Jayne received affirmative feedback, we may not always know the outcome of what we are guided to do. We must trust that we have a perfect place in the harmonious scheme of the universe. We must trust that the flow of energy—time, love, money, aid, whatever it is we are giving—goes where it is needed. We are part of a delicate and finely tuned cosmic balance. Trusting the intuition also means that we trust that we, too, will receive what we need at the right time.

Chapter Five

Cosmic Connections

OUR INTUITION DOES MUCH MORE THAN HELP US TO KEEP our lives going in the right direction. It connects us to the All That Is. Experiences of intuition can be deeply moving, even mystical.

FIELDS OF CONSCIOUSNESS

Think of the intuition as your inner desktop organizer. It is your inborn faculty that takes information perceived consciously and unconsciously, sifts through it for salient facts, and organizes it into a form that can be communicated to you in a meaningful way. This is a process that goes on within us all the time.

Not only does our intuition organize information about our daily life, it also organizes information related to the whole web of creation. Our own field of consciousness is part of bigger fields that link us to other people, even those whom we do not know and who are at a distance, and to all things, even the world of nature.

This interconnection can be seen in the concept of field consciousness. The old physics taught that objects separated by distance are isolated from one another. Quantum physics has shown us that distance is not a factor in cause and effect. Quantum fields are nonlocal; that is, they are not bounded by time and space. Neither is consciousness.

The idea that consciousness is nonlocal and exists in fields can be found in some of our oldest mystical teachings. The *Upanishads* of Hinduism put forth the idea that there is a single, cohesive underlying reality to everything—Brahman, or the Absolute Self. This single reality unfolds in fields that remain part of the whole and are connected to one another. New physics describes this whole as the implicate order.

Energy, or consciousness, is organized into fields. Morphogenetic fields are fields of energy that organize the forms and behavior of all biological, chemical, and physical systems. Once a mathematical abstraction in developmental biology, the idea of morphogenetic fields has been put forward in the last few decades as another model demonstrating that consciousness is not confined by time or space. The fields are rather like the wheel of birth, death, and rebirth, in which all things are recycled and reborn anew.

According to Rupert Sheldrake, a British plant physiologist who developed the hypothesis of morphogenetic fields, there is no end or limit to types and numbers of fields, including behavioral fields, which are responsible for coordinating instinctive or learned behavior; mental fields, which organize mental activity; social fields, which organize social behavior; and so on. Thoughts and emotions are affected by fields.

Intuition, then, functions through various morphogenetic fields, such as mental, emotional, and physical ones. These extensions of ourselves enable us to have connections with people, animals, and places, especially those that we know and care about.

Scientific research into the nature of consciousness has shown that fields of thought, focus, and intent are constantly organizing.

In *The Conscious Universe*, Dean I. Radin discusses experiments with random number generators to determine the effects of group consciousnesses established around certain events. Among them were an Academy Awards ceremony, various prime time television shows, the broadcast of the verdict in the O.J. Simpson murder trial, a small workshop, and other events. The random number generators were programmed to produce two bits of information— rather like the flipping of a coin. The results of the experiments showed that during the events, the random number generators produced an ordering of bits greater than chance. The implication of this is that group consciousness affects order in the physical world.

"The common link between mind and matter, as observed in these experiments, is *order,*" said Radin. "Order expressed in the mind is related to focused attention, and order in matter is related to decreases in randomness."[1] Radin further noted that the object of the focused attention didn't seem to be important—only that a group mind had coalesced.

In mysticism, thoughts are held to have a concrete reality to them. The power of thought can change physical reality. We attract what we think. We become what we think. The power of focused group thought has even greater power to effect change. This is psychokinesis on a large scale.

Proponents of Transcendental Meditation have attempted to demonstrate this, holding that a sufficient number of people doing Transcendental Meditation can establish more order by reducing crime, accidents, adverse weather, and so forth. There have been mass experiments to test this with intriguing results.

We are affected by changing fields of consciousness every day, in magnitudes ranging from small to large. Our intuition is an ordering function, helping us see and understand the implications of these fields—synchronicities, opportunities, problems. Intuition helps us move with the flow to our best advantage.

The result of intuitive ordering is what we often call luck.

LUCK IS BOTH MADE AND ALLOWED

We all know people who've gotten big breaks, hit jackpots, won prizes, and come up with winning ideas. With great envy, we say they're lucky: they were born under a lucky sign, the gods smiled on them, it was fate or destiny. They always seem to be in the right place at the right time.

Luck is not a matter of chance. The universe continually presents opportunities to us for growth, abundance, prosperity, and happiness. The natural order of the universe is wholeness, and we are in a constant unfoldment toward that wholeness. Our intuition is our guiding star in that unfoldment. It sifts through fields of consciousness and presents us opportunities especially in the form of warnings, nudges, and synchronicities.

Luck is what you allow to happen. That doesn't mean that you sit back, relax, and expect the universe to rain blessings upon you. You make your luck by paying attention. Lucky people pay heed to their intuition and follow it. They act on it. Lucky people *allow* their luck to unfold. They work, but they work smarter, by letting the intuition guide them to make the right move at the right time. They know when to persist and when to desist. They see potential where others do not.

When opportunities present themselves, it's not always with banners flying and trumpets blaring. It's often the opposite: a subtle signal, a slight tugging, a whisper. Some people have a natural openness to their intuition that enables them to hear the subtleties. Others have to work a little to open up. By developing your intuition, you will be better able to receive all the guidance being generated all the time by your Higher Self. You will come to *expect* luck as part of your natural order rather than be surprised by it as "chance."

REAL MAGIC

When we learn to accept our intuition and apply it—put it to work for us—we are practicing real magic.

Magic is the art of manifesting change through a projection of intent or will. The magician knows that in order to bring change in the physical realm, he must first change his consciousness. He must bring it into harmony and alignment with a Greater Consciousness.

The unfoldment of intuition brings a major change in our consciousness. We begin to see potential. We feel an expansion of our abilities, creativity, and power. We have vision and confidence in bringing vision to fruition. We sense that we have a purpose and a plan to our lives that is part of a purpose and plan to the greater whole of creation. We see that God, or the Universal Mind, is the source of all abundance and nourishment. There is no limit to that supply. Each soul has a claim to its own good, which is never diminished by the good obtained by others.

We create within us a miracle mind-set. We know that miracles are not random acts of nature or God, but the *ordered results of our change in consciousness*.

We think miracles have to be grand, dramatic events, but little miracles happen to us daily in the form of synchronicities and other ways that our intuition calls out to us. "The only qualifications for having a miracle are that one returns one's mind to peace and follows one's inner guidance," states Carolyn Miller, author of *Creating Miracles: Understanding the Experience of Divine Intervention*.[2]

CONSCIOUS INTUITION

On another level, the application of intuition is called "conscious intuition"—the ability to select the right part of our mind for whatever task, decision, or job is before us. The intuition is a balance of logic, emotion, instinct, and spiritual wisdom. In any situation, the balance may shift more toward one factor than another.

Conscious intuition is part of our evolution, what consciousness authority Robert Ornstein describes as a uniting of the insights of the rational, the emotional, the intuitive, and the spiritual:

> "The kingdom of heaven is within" and "Angels are faculties hidden in the mind of man" are ways of describing this unity. Raising consciousness means to become conscious of the different selves within and how they are partial, while also keeping aware of the larger venues of perception.[3]

We need conscious evolution if we are to learn how to survive and thrive in our global village. Conscious evolution will sharpen our skills for solving large-scale problems and for learning how to get along with our fellow human beings around the planet. Conscious evolution can take us beyond petty differences and expand our awareness so that we see situations more holistically and less selfishly.

MASTERY OF CHANGE AND TIME

Conscious intuition will be a critical skill in our ability to adapt to accelerating change. A look at the evolution of life on this planet shows that our entire history is one of shorter and shorter periods between major advancements and change. Our high technology is pushing us into shorter and shorter periods, forcing us to adapt to change more quickly. Futurists wonder about our very ability to survive as we grapple with global environmental, racial, cultural, religious, materialist, and other self-interest issues.

We will only be able to survive and thrive if we evolve on an inner basis. According to futurist Peter Russell:

> [I]f we are to survive the critical times we are now passing through, it is essential that we undergo a profound shift in

values and awaken to our inner truths and our full spiritual potential. As Buckminster Fuller put it, we are facing our final evolutionary exam. Is the human species fit to survive? Can we develop the consciousness that will allow us to use our prodigious powers with wisdom? If our civilization continues, it will be because we have passed the test, and will have already made the step into the exploration of human consciousness.[4]

Russell points out that the only obstacles to inner change are mental: our attitudes, mental habits, beliefs about what we should do and our assumptions about limitations. When we learn how to free ourselves of these fixations, we can change ourselves very rapidly.

An important key to inner change is the intuition. Intuition frees us of self-imposed limitations and notions about what we "should" do. Intuition opens us to a limitless horizon.

Businesses are awakening to the need to make fundamental changes in how they conduct their affairs in a global marketplace, where their actions have far greater ramifications than bottom line profits. In the 1970s, studies of executives showed that the most successful made use of their intuition, which they usually referred to as their gut feelings or hunches.[5] Today that intuition needs to be applied to more than marketing and product development strategies. Today's executives are increasingly concerned with a company's social and environmental responsibilities, and with employees' desires for greater work satisfaction and meaningful participation in decisions. In other words, the successful business of today and tomorrow must have heart as well as mind.

"Leadership is about creating—day by day—a domain in which human beings continually deepen their understanding of reality and are able to participate in shaping the future," says Joseph Jaworski, founder of The American Leadership Forum, a school for leaders. The ALF curriculum is designed to be an inner journey of discovery and personal renewal for corporate executives, political leaders, and leaders in all professions.

Intuition is a leadership and visionary skill that all employees from the top down need to bring to their jobs.

PEAKS AND PLATEAUS

The experience of intuition often brings an expansion, awareness, and bliss that fosters our sense of connection to things on a cosmic level. We have a peak experience. The term "peak experience" was coined by psychologist Abraham H. Maslow—the primary pioneer of humanistic and transpersonal psychologies—to describe nonreligious quasi-mystical and mystical experiences. Peak experiences are a sudden flash of intense happiness and feelings of well-being, and perhaps awareness of "ultimate truth" and the unity of all things. They are accompanied by a heightened sense of control over the body and emotions, and a wider sense of awareness, as though one is standing on a mountaintop. They foster a sense of being lucky or graced; release creative energies; reaffirm the worthiness of life; and change an individual's view of himself.

Maslow described peak experiences as having "a special flavor of wonder, of awe, of reverence, of humility, and surrender . . ." The individual, he said, feels "one with the world, pleased with it, really belonging to it, instead of being on the outside looking in . . . they had really seen the ultimate truth, the essence of things . . ."[6]

These same phenomena can flood us in intuitive experiences as well. It is important for us to have such experiences, for they facilitate the achievement of our full potential. According to Maslow, every human being has innate spiritual yearnings to experience the sacred and fulfill himself to his maximum potential of goodness in terms of healthy living, honesty, creativity, compassion, unselfishness, and so on. Those who do so become "self-actualized": they are mature, healthy, and filled with a zest for living. They have successfully integrated their lower instinctual nature with their higher, godlike nature.

Developing our intuition helps us to accomplish self-actualization. Intuitive experiences are often peak experiences. The intuition opens the heart and expands our worldview. Using our intuition requires an integration and balancing of our lower and higher natures.

Using our intuition expands our creativity in all aspects of life. Maslow said that a self-actualized person is happier, healthier, and more creative. Interestingly, he did not equate creativity with great talent, but merely with an ability to do anything, even routine things, creatively.

Maslow said that self-actualized people are more likely to have peak experiences. He coined the term "plateau experience" to describe a sort of continuing peak experience throughout life.

YOUR LIFE WILL CHANGE FOR THE BETTER

Intuition is holistic—it draws from, addresses, and affects all parts of our being. It is the wisdom of the heart. If you have a sincere desire to become more intuitive, be prepared for your entire life to change. You cannot bring intuition to your job, for example, without intuition spilling over into your personal life and your spiritual outlook. If you begin by viewing intuition strictly as a mental discipline to increase your brain power, you will not contain it there. At some point you will become more sensitive to others, empathically picking up on their thoughts, feelings, and moods. At some point you will become aware of a "higher power" beyond you that has a hand in your life. Intuition requires an open heart, and you cannot open your heart without becoming more concerned for and involved with your fellow human beings. You cannot open your heart without pondering— and experiencing—a profound connection to the Creator.

That's as it should be. Intuition is part of our path of evolution, our soul growth. It combines the best of our instinctual, emotional, and rational brains with our spiritual awareness. I look upon my own intuition as a team effort. I can't take all the credit for my intuition, for that would deny the presence of the spiritual. I can't project my intuition solely onto spiritual beings, for that would deny my own contributions of consciousness. My intuition comes from within me, that is, my Higher Self, and also from without as divine intercession. I feel the guiding hand of angels, saints, and the Creator.

Alan Seale, a minister, spiritual/clairvoyant counselor, singer, and modern mystic, sees intuition as inseparable from one's spiritual journey. It takes us into our deep inner wisdom where we know our oneness with All:

> At its highest level, the intuitive voice is the part of you that is one with the great mystery, that is Love. It is the voice of God within. Intuitive awareness develops hand-in-hand with your willingness to step beyond the intellectual mind, so that you may know and *experience* the infinite possibilities that exist beyond the bounds of ordinary consciousness. The way to this inner wisdom is through your own personal spiritual and mystical journey—embracing this inner voice as Spirit, and allowing it to the few as teacher, counselor, guide, and friend.[7]

This inner voice of spirit is the foundation of mystical life.

The mystical life is a deepening relationship with Spirit or God. We do not have to be monks in a monastery to have mysticism as part of our lives. When we seek our highest potential, when we strive to the highest ideals, when we open our hearts to others, we are walking the mystical path.

As a psychotherapist, Belleruth Naparstek naturally brings a great deal of empathy to her job. She found that by having an open heart, her intuition fosters a profound connection to others that benefits the therapy:

> . . . I'm so empathically attuned to my clients when I'm in this state, seeing what they see and feeling what they feel, that I'm aware of an overall, generalized feeling of what I can only describe as *love* for them. I'm so suffused with it, I am easily moved by what they say or do with it. (This doesn't mean I'm not thinking clearly; on the contrary, my thinking is clearer than usual. At the same time, I am deeply touched by them in this generalized way.) And, where elsewhere in my life I might be critical of their behavior or find fault with their attitudes, in this state compassion crowds out judgment. This doesn't take effort—if it did, I'm sure I'd feel virtuous about it—it just happens.
>
> And most of all, I feel very alive—very present and deeply grateful to be doing this work that I do. A quiet elation fills me as I sit at what has somehow become a glorious kind of meditation.[8]

All of us can experience this love and aliveness. Intuition increases our empathy and compassion and reduces our tendency to criticize and judge. Thus, our relationships to others improve and take on new dimensions and nuances. What's more, when we feel genuine love for others, we experience the miracle of more love flowing back to us.

Says Naparstek:

> And from the open heart, we get the true picture of exactly who and what we are. This view is stunning. We've become an enormous energy field that has instantaneous reach everywhere.[9]

Intuition truly raises us to a higher level of being. The writings of our great thinkers throughout history, whether they were scientists, politicians, businessmen, or mystics, all acknowledge that behind their inspirations is the presence of the Divine.

Chapter Six

The Holistic Intuitive Lifestyle

THE EXERCISES IN THIS BOOK WILL HELP YOU TO DEVELOP and polish your intuitive skills. But there is more than mental exercises to becoming intuitive. Using your intuition is part of a holistic approach to living. Like plants that flourish when they receive enough light, water, and nutrients, intuition flourishes when we nourish all parts of our life—when we are as healthy and vital as possible physically, mentally, emotionally, and spiritually.

I recommend that you integrate the following nine-point plan into your daily and regular activities:

1. GET REGULAR PHYSICAL EXERCISE

Getting regular physical exercise enhances our health on all four levels, of course. Exercise is especially important for intuition. When you exert yourself, especially in a rhythmic activity, you breathe more deeply. This circulates energy throughout your auric field and benefits the chakras. As noted in the exercises in Part II, breathing techniques are fundamental to stimulating the intuition.

A profound change in consciousness can happen to us when we exercise, perhaps due to the chemicals released in the brain. Remember that I observed that I often have my best inspirations while exercising on a stationary bicycle.

Athletes are well aware of this shift and many have reported unusual psychic and mystical phenomena while immersed in their performance. They enter a state of consciousness called "the zone," in which time and space are unbounded. When in the zone, they excel in what they are doing. The zone also is where the intuition exists—there are no limits to what can be perceived in time and space.

These experiences have been well documented by Michael Murphy, cofounder of The Esalen Institute in Big Sur, California, and Rhea A. White, parapsychologist, reference librarian, and founder of the Exceptional Human Experience Network. White coined the term "exceptional human experience" to describe 150 types of anomalous, nonordinary experiences of a psychic, mystical, and transcendent nature.

In 1972, Murphy published his book *Golf in the Kingdom*, which describes such experiences reported by people while they played golf. In response to the interest in that book, Murphy and White teamed to write *The Psychic Side of Sports*, published in 1978, and revised and reissued as *In the Zone: Transcendent Experience in Sports*, in 1995. They documented some sixty phenomena that occur in more than twenty types of experiences in the zone. Among them are:

- feelings of power and superiority

- acute well-being and calm

- ecstasy; unity

- altered perceptions of time and space

- psi

- out-of-body experiences

- perceptions of "the other" (such as spirit beings)

- the ability to exert mind over matter, or psychokinesis

In all, Murphy and White found striking similarities in the extraordinary powers unleashed by sport activity and the extraordinary powers, or *siddhis,* developed through the practice of yoga.

But do you have to be a professional or world-class athlete to receive such benefits, particularly for your intuition?

Not at all. Recall that Einstein was inspired when he sailed or canoed, and Mozart was inspired when he walked in the woods after dinner. Gardening has opened the inspiration doorways for myself and many others.

However, you shouldn't undertake physical exercise with the idea that you *will* or *must* have an exceptional experience. Even running a marathon is no guarantee that an exceptional experience will happen. Holding such an intent defeats the purpose of exercising, which (besides improved health) is to allow the mind to shift gears and enter an open space.

Pick an activity you like and exercise for the sheer joy of it. Allow the rest—the intuition and the inspiration—to occur in the right time and place. Sometimes the intuitive flash comes after the exercise.

Of course, follow whatever medical advice is appropriate for you.

In concert with your exercise program, pay attention to your nutrition so that you are at peak energy. That also means getting adequate rest. It's hard for the intuition to hammer its way through a mental haze created by fatigue. Alcohol and caffeine, especially consumed at night, can disrupt sleep patterns.

Many of us have sensitivities and allergies to certain foods and to the chemical additives in packaged and junk food. These can affect our energy level, mental clarity, and overall health. If you suspect you have food sensitivities or allergies, you may want to consult the appropriate health care practitioner.

2. MEDITATE DAILY

Meditation is the stilling of the mind. Primarily a spiritual discipline for spiritual advancement, meditation also has health benefits. Studies show that regular practice of meditation lowers the body's metabolism, slows brain waves, and induces relaxation. Individuals who meditate regularly show greater resistance to stress and illness and feel better psychologically.[1]

All of these results produced by meditation are beneficial to the intuition. It is in that stillness that the intuition manifests. And we have an easier time accessing intuition when we are feeling our best. As noted in the previous chapter, meditation facilitates the highest expression of mystical intuition as well as intuition related to everyday matters.

There are many techniques for meditation, and students of various spiritual paths can spend years in their practice, perfecting posture, breathing, use of mantra, and transcendence of thought. For years I studied Zen meditation. Though I am much more casual in my approach to meditation today, I still incorporate some of what I learned from Zen into my personal practice.

If you follow a particular school, continue to use it. If you have not been a meditator, don't be daunted by the thought that you have to learn a complicated system. You can meditate simply by sitting quietly in a chair and quieting the mind. If you do this for even a few minutes every day, you will soon begin to notice changes in your state of well-being, your awareness and perception of what goes on around you—and your intuition. You will become more tuned into subtleties.

As we have seen, detachment is necessary for intuition. We must be detached from outcomes in order to receive the true guidance. Meditation helps us to detach from worldly concerns and hear the voice within.

Meditation exercises for expanding the intuition are given in Key #2 in Part II.

3. PRAY DAILY

Prayer brings the same benefits as meditation. In fact, it is difficult to differentiate between the two. Most prayer involves communication and dialogue with a higher power, which also constitute a form of meditation called active meditation. Sometimes we sit in silence in prayer, quieting the mind to hear what Spirit has to say to us. In this form, prayer is more like the concentration meditation of the East.

Prayer is an attunement to God or Divine Mind, which holds the perfection of all things. In the terms of physics, it is the bridge to the implicate order.

In prayer, we seek to tap into the currents of Divine Mind for help and guidance. Our intuitive faculty brings us the answers. Like regular meditators, regular pray-ers know that prayer improves their overall well-being, psychological outlook, and intuitive ability. Positive effects have been documented in scientific studies.[2]

As the author of four books on the power of prayer, I have experienced firsthand and been witness to many examples of the dramatic changes prayer can make in life. It's a must for the spiritual, holistic, intuitive life.

We may make excuses why we don't meditate (we can't find the time, we don't have a good space), but there is no excuse for not praying. Prayer can be done anywhere and anytime.

Prayer also builds faith. It certainly builds faith in a religious or spiritual sense, but it is important in all areas of life. Faith strengthens our trust in our intuition, the guidance that comes through the intuition, and our ability to put the guidance into action.

The best definition of faith can be found in the Bible, in Hebrews 11:1: "Now faith is the assurance of things hoped for, the conviction of things not seen." The intuition puts us in touch with the unseen, the potential, the unmanifest that awaits our action. The intuition tells us what our physical senses do not perceive, and what known fact does not necessarily support. It calls us to certain actions that the rational thought cautions, "Wait a moment! Where's the evidence?" The intuition gives us a vision of the possible. Faith gives us the fuel to make the vision real.

Faith is especially evident in creativity. Artistic genius, inventions, and risk-taking would not be possible without faith. Innovation and risk-taking in business would not be possible without faith.

Visionaries of all kinds are ridiculed by others. Faith makes it possible to withstand ridicule and persevere. Inventions that we cannot imagine life without today were disparaged once by the visionless as ridiculous, stupid, and a waste of money: the automobile, the photocopying machine, the telephone, and the typewriter, to name just a few.

In the 1920s, a man named DeWitt Wallace had a vision to publish a monthly magazine digest of the best articles that had appeared in other magazines. His intuition told him it would be a big hit. The problem was, he lacked money to start up a publishing operation. He approached others, including the giants of the publishing industry, for financial backing. Every one of them turned him down. They told him his idea was worthless, and that if he was foolish enough to pursue it, he would wind up bankrupt. But Wallace had faith in his intuition. He set up a modest publishing business in his garage. Thus was born *Readers' Digest*, which grew into a multibillion-dollar international publishing powerhouse.

Our intuition needs the support of our faith. Prayer builds faith.

It's especially important to end your day with prayer—or meditation—to clear your mind of negative thoughts. Your thoughts are the creative fuel to your Higher Self. If you think negative, destructive thoughts, they will become your building blocks of life. When you clear and purify your thoughts with prayer or meditation, you generate a much higher and positive energy. Your intuition cannot function well in a consciousness of fear, anger, and negativity. It functions best in a consciousness of peace, self-confidence, love, and harmony. You will attract what you think. Think and pray well.

4. MAINTAIN MINDFULNESS

Centuries ago, the great artist Raphael told the great artist and inventor Leonardo da Vinci, "I have noticed that when one paints, one should think of nothing: everything then comes better."[3]

Raphael was expressing the value of mindfulness. When he painted, Raphael did not allow himself to become distracted with thoughts about anything other than what he was doing. In thinking "of nothing," he was focusing his full attention upon his art, and all of his energy thus flowed directly onto the canvas.

Most of us live nearly our entire lives somewhere else besides the present. We rehash the past and anticipate the future. All we ever have, however, is *now*. By not living in the now, by not giving ourselves fully to the moment, we let life pass us by.

Mindfulness means devoting yourself to one thing at a time. It means being fully present in what you are doing. Today we rush around, pressed for time, trying to do several things at once. We do paperwork over lunch, shave while we drive, listen to an audio book on a headset while we grocery shop. Everything gets a fragment of our attention. Does acting like an octopus really make life better? No, we complain more than ever about how pressed we are. We look for ways to become busier, to do more faster. No wonder we can't hear our intuition.

Intuition is a product of the now. It lives in the still point within. Make a commitment to live more in the moment. As you go about your daily affairs, give them your total attention. You will be surprised how much time you spend doing things you do not want to do, but feel obliged to do, or how much time you spend in unproductive activity. When you realize how precious the moment is, you will exercise more care over how you spend your time. You will feel better for it, and become more productive. Being centered and in the moment creates conditions in which intuition can flourish.

I was in the habit of using driving time as thinking time: sorting, planning, plotting, brainstorming, and so on. It's also worry time: worry about this, worry about that. A turning point came one day when I set out for an hour's drive to an appointment. I had a lot on my mind. An organization in the throes of internal upheaval and divisiveness had asked me to come and give an inspirational talk and workshop to help their healing process. I wanted to compose some new material that would be right on target for them. I had gone round and round with many ideas, but none of them clicked for me. I had tried some intuitive brainstorming techniques, but a breakthrough had yet to come. Even though I was in the verge of overthinking the matter, I normally would have used this driving time to think some more about it.

Instead, I reminded myself of mindfulness. I resolved that I would not think about anything but driving. Soon I was in a peaceful state of mind. I focused on the feel of the steering wheel in my hands, on the sense of motion as the car moved along the freeway, the feel and sounds of the road. I appreciated the technology that made it possible for me to cover long distances in a relatively short amount of time. I appreciated being out on the road on a sunny spring day.

Suddenly, into the midst of this bliss flashed the solution I'd been trying so hard to get. It was a brand-new idea, and it fell into my head completely developed. I was elated. At the same time, I felt a deep and profound connection to everything around me.

Mindfulness also helps you to let go of your attachments to emotions, especially negative ones such as anger, fear, and guilt. Negative emotions inhibit your access to your intuition. When you live in a state of mindfulness, you can observe the emotions and release them, much the same as you observe thoughts and release them in meditation. Many emotional attachments belong to events or circumstances long past that we keep replaying in our minds. By living more in the moment, you will be less likely to carry emotional attachments around with you.

In Zen, mindfulness is "seeing with the whole mind." We see everything as it really is without effort. We think without effort. Wisdom comes out of mindfulness.

5. ENJOY A BEGINNER'S MIND

What does it mean to have a beginner's mind? In Zen, it is one of the fundamentals to starting the spiritual work.

Our fast-paced lives bring a been-there-done-that jaded weariness. We are full of expectations, disappointments, cautions, and ambitions that pile up higher and higher as we go through life. We see fewer and fewer possibilities and opportunities. Once upon a time, life seemed much easier. If only we could turn back the clock and start over again.

All it takes to revitalize your outlook on the world is beginner's mind.

Beginner's mind constantly sees the world as new. Instead of limit there is limitlessness. Instead of doubt there is openness. No matter how often something is done—a task, a chore, the recitation of a prayer—the beginner's mind experiences it as if for the first time every time, knowing that no two experiences are ever the same.

Wayne W. Dyer describes this as a sense of total and complete awe. When we practice being in awe daily—holding a reverence for all life and giving thanks for what we take for granted—we soon enter a state of enlightenment. "Enlightenment is simply the silent acceptance and appreciation for what is," Dyer says. "Be enlightened and miracles will be your way of life."[4]

Beginner's mind is akin to the archetype of The Fool. The Fool is not a person who is ignorant and reckless, but a person who is willing to be open to all possibilities. The Fool has no prejudices, no habits. The Fool looks out on a world of unbounded opportunity and adventure. He has a natural mind and is constantly filled with wonder.

This doesn't mean that the lessons and wisdom of experience should be dismissed. But if we keep our outlook fresh and open, we are more vibrant, more expressive, more creative, more inventive. We see our place and our importance in the whole cosmic scheme of things. Intuition expands within us.

Mindfulness and beginner's mind go hand in hand.

6. APPRECIATE NATURE

Make it a point to spend some time in nature as often as possible. Sit outdoors during lunch, go for a walk in a park, spend a weekend in the mountains or at the seashore. Nature is conducive to peak and mystical experiences. The great philosopher William James was fifty-seven years old when he went hiking in the Adirondack mountains. There, he was swept up in spiritual experiences that he described as a meeting in his breast between all the gods of the nature mythologies and the moral gods of the inner life. He intuited truths that had eluded him intellectually. The experiences inspired much of the content of his classic work,

The Varieties of Religious Experience: A Study in Human Nature, and also stimulated his interest in the paranormal.

When you are out in nature, practice mindfulness and beginner's mind. Experience everything around you as though for the first time. Take in your environment through your senses, one by one. Gaze at a flower and appreciate its beauty in detail. Think no particular thoughts, but enjoy what nature has to offer.

The great inventor Michael Faraday credited some of his greatest intuitive leaps to time spent in nature doing "idle woolgathering" that had no object other than pleasure:

> A sensitive mind will always acknowledge the pleasures it receives from a luxuriant prospect of nature; the beautiful mingling and gradations of color, the delicate perspective, the ravishing effect of light and shade, and the fascinating variety and grace of the outline, must be seen to be felt; for expressions can never convey the ecstatic joy they give to the imagination, or the benevolent feeling they create in the mind. There is no boundary, there is no restraint 'til reason draws the rein.[5]

In addition, practice the Expanded Listening exercise described in Key #6 in Part II. The exercise will help you listen to the subtle undercurrents of nature.

7. READ SPIRITUAL LITERATURE

The great sacred texts of the world's religions and philosophies provide super-rich nutrients for the intuition. They embody our highest ideals, ethics, values, and understandings of Truth.

In addition, the writings of the world's great mystics contain a powerful spiritual force that opens up the consciousness. Mystics write from an intense level of inspiration, intuition, and Truth—they are literally pens in the hand of God. So inspired are they that some mystics seem difficult to comprehend, at least with left-brain thinking. To get the most out of the mystics, one should approach them from an intuitive standpoint in an open, receptive frame of mind. The wisdom of the mystics is absorbed rather than learned. In an alchemical fashion, it sinks deep into consciousness, where it works and bubbles away to later burst forth in an illumined thought, inspiration, or revelation.

Spiritual literature trains our consciousness to be receptive to the Divine Mind. As the medieval German mystic Jakob Boehme said:

> When both thy intellect and will are quiet and passive to the
> expressions of the eternal Word and Spirit, and when thy
> soul is winged up above that which is temporal, the outward
> senses and the imagination being locked up by holy abstrac-
> tion, *then* the eternal Hearing, Seeing, and Speaking will be
> revealed in thee.[6]

Pick a sacred text or collection of mystical writings (there are many "user-friendly" translations of the mystics available in print) and keep it as a bedside companion. Read a little every night before you sleep. You will finish your day and enter your night in a much more relaxed state. And, you will fertilize the field of your dreams, another rich source of intuitive guidance.

If mystical writings seem too heavy, select a collection of light inspirational writings.

8. PAY ATTENTION TO YOUR DREAMS

As we saw earlier, the intuition often speaks through dreams. I have done dreamwork for the better part of my life, and I believe that dreams are one of our best and richest sources of spiritual, creative, and practical guidance. The intuition uses dreams to get across powerful messages and great ideas.

We all dream nightly, and we have multiple dreams throughout our sleep cycle. Most of us remember only the dream we are having prior to waking up. Some people naturally have sharper dream recall than others. Some have a difficult time remembering dreams, and may think they do not dream at all. However, scientific research has demonstrated that we do dream, whether we remember them or not.

Your dreams are a voice of your Higher Self. Simply acknowledging dreams and asking them to reveal more to you will often stimulate a response of increased dream awareness and recall.

Many people don't pay much attention to their dreams because on the surface they seem rather strange and inscrutable. Yet dreams reveal themselves quite easily when we catch on to how they communicate. Dreams speak in symbols and images. Sometimes their meaning is quite obvious to us. Other times we can use a variety of techniques such as free association and meanings of universal symbols to help us interpret them.

I find dreams to be quite rewarding in insight. Dreams are mirrors of Truth. They make use of images from daily life—things we have done recently—and also draw upon archetypal images as well. Every intuitive should have an understanding of his or her dream life in order to get the full benefit of intuition. There isn't space in this book to present a comprehensive dream program. Many books are available to help you with recall and interpretation. I recommend that you take a look at my books *Dreamwork for the Soul* and *The Encyclopedia of Dreams*.

Try the dream incubation in Key #12 in Part II to learn how to ask your dreams for specific guidance.

9. USE MUSIC MEDICINE

Our holistic diet for the intuition includes a sound diet as well. The powerful effects of music upon mind, body, and spirit have been known and used since ancient times. Modern research is demonstrating what our distant ancestors already knew: music heals, inspires, soothes, and opens the gateways to breakthrough experiences.

The ancient Chinese believed music to be the basis of everything: all things, including man, were molded according to the music that was performed within them. Confucius stated that if the music of a kingdom changed, then its society would alter itself accordingly. Plato, too, believed that music had the power to affect the fortunes of a nation. The Greeks used music extensively in healing.

Modern studies have documented how music affects biochemical and hormonal processes and neuromuscular activity, and suppresses pain-conducting structures in the brain stem. Music therapy is used to treat a wide range of physical and psychological conditions and to treat pain. Music also can help to induce altered states of consciousness that produce peak and mystical experiences and intuitive flashes of insight and creativity. It can help us to absorb more information when we read.

Chris works as a creative writer for a large advertising agency. When her company landed a prize new client, she was assigned to the account. It was a plum opportunity for her, but one that made her anxious and nervous about performing. She struggled with ideas for the print campaign. Nothing seemed to hit. Her wastebasket piled up with discarded ideas. One day she went home mentally exhausted, unable to give the account another thought. While she prepared dinner, she listened to classical music. Soon she was pleasantly distracted, carried away by the music while she sliced her vegetables. Suddenly it burst upon her: the breakthrough revelation for the campaign. As it flashed into her mind, she "knew" without a doubt that it would be successful.

Researchers have discovered that the music of Mozart is particularly beneficial to well-being and creativity. As musicologist Don Campbell reports in *The Mozart Effect*, "the rhythms, melodies and high frequencies of Mozart's music stimulate and charge the creative and motivational regions of the brain."[7]

Musicology is a fascinating topic and is well worth a little study to learn more about how sound and vibration affect us. Too often, we are mindless about the sounds with which we surround ourselves. We turn on music more as background noise, and we often think the louder it is the better. While music has been shown to help us, studies also show that the wrong kind of sound and music—especially loud, discordant sounds and heavy, low vibrations of sounds—can adversely affect our health.

Music is part of our holistic diet, a potential source of nourishment for the body, mind, spirit—and intuition.

Here are nine points for using music to enhance your intuition:

- *Work with music you like.* Play familiar music that pleases you and reflects the mood you want to be in. Avoid music that has unhappy or negative associations. Learn how different pieces energize you or relax you. Generally, music that will lower your pulse rate has a beat of sixty pulses per minute or less, is played on strings and woodwinds and has no lyrics. Music that is more stimulating has a faster tempo and has prominent brass and drums. Lyrics stimulate by engaging emotions and thought processes. All classical music is not automatically relaxing—if it has a fast tempo, it can stimulate as much as some rock music.

- *Pay attention to your breathing and body.* When music relaxes you, your breathing becomes deeper and more regular. If your breathing becomes shallow or irregular, the music is agitating your body. If you feel pain, discomfort, music is having a negative affect.

- *Take music baths.* Music is most effective when it is experienced in its fullness. Rather than play music only as background for activity, set aside time regularly to do nothing but listen to music with total awareness. Think of the music as washing over you. Breathe into the music, let your body be carried by it. Become one of the instruments. When you're done, you'll feel light, energized, and relaxed.

▪ *Keep a musical notebook.* By recording how different types of music and individual compositions affect you physically, emotionally, and spiritually, you will gain a better understanding of the impact of music on your health. Keep a discography of composers and selections and your response to them.

▪ *Take a "sound inventory" of your home.* The body reacts to all sounds around it. Music will be much more effective if you minimize or eliminate distracting noises such as appliances and outside sounds. Take your music baths in the quietest room in the house. Use music to mask noises you cannot reduce or eliminate.

▪ *Use imagery and positive thinking.* Music can enhance your energy and creativity if you give yourself positive suggestions and affirmations while listening to appropriate selections. Visualize yourself accomplishing a goal. If you're faced with a problem, ask for help. The answer may come to you while you listen. If relaxation is your goal, visualize your favorite peaceful setting.

▪ *Let music enhance your daily activities.* To get off to a fresh and brisk start each morning, play music with a lively rhythm. Household chores will be less tedious if done to a lively beat. Unwind at the end of the day with selections that are soft and soothing. Play relaxing music during dinner to aid digestion. Listen to more relaxing music just before you retire to help you sink into a deep and peaceful slumber.

▪ *Let music enhance your prayer or meditation.* You may prefer to pray or meditate in silence, but music can deepen the experience by preparing you for silence—quieting your mind and body and allowing you to be more receptive to the Divine. Such pieces are discovered over time and through careful listening. Used regularly for prayer or meditation, they can help you attain a receptive state of mind much more quickly.

- *Play a musical instrument.* Many of us learn to play an instrument in childhood, then give it up later in life. Something extra happens when you play a musical instrument that does not occur just by listening. The instrument and music become part of you. And, most instruments require a certain amount of arm movement or deep breathing, which is good exercise. It doesn't matter if you aren't a professional-caliber musician. Play for the sheer pleasure and beauty of music.

⌐ PART II

Keys for Developing Your Intuition

Introduction to the Keys

THIS SECTION FEATURES TWENTY-TWO KEYS, OR TOOLS, which comprise a comprehensive plan to open, increase, and hone your intuitive skill. Within the keys are multiple exercises. In all, there are ninety-four exercises in this book.

Each Key has its own unique role in your intuitive unfoldment. Most of them can be done by yourself. A few require partners.

Keys one through twelve cover different approaches to the intuition and get you comfortable with expanding your unseen senses. Keys thirteen through twenty-two are especially helpful for improving your accuracy.

You will excel at some techniques more than others. Go through all the Keys before you settle on the techniques you wish to work with the most. Incorporate the Keys into your holistic, intuitive living.

(Note: Opening the intuition can bring up material from the subconscious that may require professional assistance. Individuals presently in therapy should consult with their practitioners before undertaking exercises in this book. Individuals with respiratory, heart, or other medical conditions should consult with their doctors before doing the breathing exercises in Key #1, Exercise #2: "The Alchemical Breath.")

Intuitive Breathing

THE FIRST AND MOST IMPORTANT THING YOU CAN LEARN IN developing your intuition is a good breathing technique. If you meditate or practice yoga, or if you have read any literature about Eastern medicine, then you understand that the breath is not just the medium for taking oxygen into the body, but serves as the medium for the universal life force, which governs health and well-being. In metaphysics, the universal life force is a substance that permeates all things. It is known as prana, chi, ki, mana and other terms. When our ability to absorb universal life force is good, we are healthy and vital. When our ability to absorb it becomes poor or impaired, our health suffers. Good breathing techniques help to distribute and circulate the universal life force throughout the body.

The universal life force also penetrates both the body and the aura through the chakras, whirlpool-like interfaces. We have numerous chakras, but there are seven primary ones, which are aligned approximately along the spine. Each chakra governs physical, emotional, and spiritual functions, including those that relate to good intuition. Breathing techniques help to keep the chakras clear and open.

Numerous breathing techniques have been developed, especially in the Eastern arts of meditation and medicine. Some of them are quite complicated. I have tried a variety of them myself, sitting or standing in certain positions, breathing through alternate nostrils, holding my tongue in certain positions, and so on. Most of them didn't seem to be all that practical.

EXERCISE #1: THE INTUITIVE BREATH

This technique is so simple you can do it anywhere. Take three long, slow and deep breaths. Breathe in through your nostrils. You can either breathe out through your nostrils or your mouth. As you breathe, focus on these:

1. Breathe . . . *slow down*.

When we're trying to solve a problem or make a decision or get ideas, our mind races. Thoughts run in all directions. The first breath is to rein in that distraction.

2. Breathe . . . *center*.

Pull in your energy and focus the breath in the body. Be fully present in the moment. The second breath is to gather your inner resources.

3. Breathe . . . *release and expand*.

As you exhale on the third breath, be aware that the Higher Self is now in charge. Space has been made in your consciousness for intuition to reveal what you need to know.

In three breaths, you will find yourself remarkably composed and in a different state of consciousness. The Intuitive Breath employs a little esoteric magic as well. In numbers mysticism, three represents the ascent of consciousness to higher planes. It's a door-opener to the realm of spirit. When we use the number three with a mindfulness in meditative exercises, we are seeking higher wisdom. This is why we find three so often in tales of mysticism and magic: charms are recited three times; we are given three wishes; and so on.

Think of the Intuitive Breath as represented by the upward-pointing triangle that rests on the earth (the physical plane) and points to the heavens (intuitive wisdom). The breath brings our mind, body, and spirit into harmony and balance so that the heavens can be reached.

EXERCISE #2: THE ALCHEMICAL BREATH

Then I learned one simple technique that made me a believer in the role of breathing in the development of the intuition. I found that when I used it, my sixth sense opened more quickly and with greater sensitivity. The more I used it, the faster I progressed. What's more, the simplicity of it encouraged me to use it daily, anywhere or any time, sitting or standing, alone or in the midst of people. I call it the Alchemical Breath because it reminds me of old alchemical images that depict the circulation of vital energies between heaven and earth in the process of wholeness and enlightenment.

Alchemy is a Western mystery path of enlightenment. We tend to think of alchemists as persons who tried to turn lead into gold. Many of them did indeed pursue that, but the physical gold was a metaphor for the spiritual gold of enlightenment, attained through processes of purification. The development of the intuition is part of alchemy, as it is any path of enlightenment.

The original purpose for which I learned this breathing technique was bioenergy healing. My teacher, Mietek Wirkus, taught it as a way to quickly raise the level of the universal life force for the purpose of healing through the hands. Energy healing involves sensing and working with the subtle energies of the chakras and aura, which must be done on an intuitive level. Out of all of the breathing techniques I have ever tried, I like this one the best. Here's how it works:

Imagine that you are in an oval bubble. As you breathe in and out, you will visualize yourself pushing the breath up and down and around this bubble, anchored around chakra points.

The starting point is the root chakra at the back of the spine. As the breath is drawn in, visualize it traveling up the spine to the base of the back of the head. Then hold the breath briefly and visualize it traveling from the base of the head to the forehead, the point of the sixth chakra. As the breath is exhaled, visualize it pouring from the sixth chakra down the front of the body back to the root chakra. Hold the breath briefly again, and visualize pushing from the front of the root chakra to the back. Breathe in and start the circulation cycle over again.

All of the breathing is done through the nostrils. Inhale deeply into the belly. When you exhale, push the breath out from the belly. As it exits through the nostrils, allow it to rattle at the back of the palate, as though you were going to make a snorting noise.

The inhalation, exhalation, and holding of the breath is done in a ratio of two to one: 4/2, 6/3, or 8/4. For example, breathe in for the count of eight, hold the breath for the count of four, breathe out for the count of eight, hold the breath for the count of four, and so on.

The shorter the ratio cycle, the faster the universal life force is circulated, and the faster the energy is raised. In the beginning, it is good to practice with an 8/4 or 6/3 ratio. When you are comfortable with the technique, try the 4/2 ratio.

Okay, are you ready to give it a try?

Stand with your spine straight. Relax your body. Become aware of your breathing. Most of us breathe too shallowly. You will probably find that your breath doesn't go down into the belly. Take a few deep breaths and push the air down as far as possible, expanding your belly as you breathe in.

Place your point of concentration at the root chakra. Now breathe deeply and begin the cycle with a count of eight. Pull the breath energy up the spine counting to eight . . . hold the breath and push the energy from the back of the head through the third eye counting four . . . expell the breath down to the root chakra counting eight . . . hold the breath and push from the front of the root chakra to the back counting four . . . and being again.

Do the entire cycle three times.

How do you feel? If you are not accustomed to breathing deeply, you may feel a little tingling sensation or some light-headedness. These sensations will diminish the more you practice. Take your time and go at a comfortable pace.

Do ten complete cycles. You should feel refreshed and energized. Some people feel some discomfort, even a slight headache. This may be due to the circulation of sluggish energy in the sixth chakra. Again, the more you practice this breathing technique, the more such symptoms are likely to diminish.

Now that you understand the process, focus on the element that will benefit the circulation of energy in the third eye. As you exhale, rattle the breath in the back of the palate, as though you were going to exhale through the mouth, but push the breath out through the nostrils instead. Continue to visualize the breath energy pouring out of the third eye on the exhale.

Do five more cycles.

Give yourself a little rest. Now try the breathing to a shorter counting cycle: 6/3. Breathe in and out to a count of six and hold the breath to a count of three. Do three complete cycles.

Give yourself another little rest. This time, shorten the counting cycle to 4/2. Do three complete cycles. You will notice that the longer counting cycles make you feel more relaxed, while the short cycle raises a lot of energy. Healers who use this breathing technique often do the short cycle as a way of maximizing the flow of energy to the patient. For the purposes of intuition, I find that the longer cycles work better. I use the 6/3 most often. Over time, you will find that you no longer need to keep a precise count, but do the breathing naturally.

The Alchemical Breath can be done either standing or sitting. Do ten cycles to start the day. It's also a good idea to do a few Alchemical Breaths throughout the day, such as when you are standing in line or sitting at a desk. It's a great way to refresh your energy and concentration at any time. Of course, do a few breaths before undertaking an intuition exercise. But if you simply use this breathing technique on a daily basis, you'll find your intuition clearer and more responsive all of the time.

Meditation Adventures

BREATHING TECHNIQUES AND REGULAR MEDITATION ARE the two most important activities you can do to encourage the expansion of your intuitive mind. If you think that meditation requires you to be a loin-clothed, fasting yogi sitting for hours in a lotus position, you've got the wrong impression. There are many styles of meditation. You can make it enjoyable and interesting, even if you spend only fifteen or twenty minutes at it. For the best results and the fastest progress, daily is the ideal frequency. If you're not in the habit of daily meditation, do it as often as you can every week. It's not an all-or-nothing proposition. Once you start and see the benefits of it, you'll want to meditate daily.

You don't need a special room, clothing, mats, or cushions. Wear your regular clothing and use a comfortable chair or sofa for seating. It is helpful to have a quiet place. If you have a busy family, find a spot in an unused room or go into your bedroom.

I find that meditation in the morning is best. It is worth getting up a little earlier in order to do it. Meditation freshens the mind, calms, and centers, and is a great way to start the day. Nighttime prior to sleep is also good. Many people find time to meditate during their workday, such as lunch breaks. They close the door to their office or find a spot outdoors. Some even sit in their cars. I have meditated many times on planes, trains, and buses.

The purpose of meditation is to still the mind so that one can achieve a breakthrough of consciousness to a higher spiritual level. From the standpoint of the intuition, meditation stills the busy mind and clears the decks for the breakthrough of insight.

Meditation uplifts the mind and soul so that we are functioning on the highest possible level of being. Regardless of how you wish to use your intuition, know that it is coming from a source of divine Truth. The higher we set our sights, the clearer the guidance for our best good.

Meditation is like planting and fertilizing a crop. For a while, it seems that nothing happens. Then suddenly new growth sprouts above the surface.

Meditation also will take you below the surface into your own depths. The results of that journeying—the crop of intuitive insights—will spring forth at the appropriate time.

Sometimes, however, meditations do spontaneously take on a life of their own. When that happens, go with them and allow them to unfold. You may find yourself hearing, seeing, or being shown or given things. Accept, acknowledge, observe. Analyze and interpret later.

At the end of every exercise, always give thanks for the experience. Intuitive results may not be apparent immediately, but they will unfold. Gratitude is empowering. It acknowledges our gifts from within and from the realm of spirit.

EXERCISE #1: SITTING MEDITATION

Sit in a comfortable place. (You will remain more alert if you are seated. Lying down, you may become so relaxed that you fall asleep.) Keep your spine as straight as possible. Allow the body to relax by breathing deeply and slowly. Use intuitive breathing.

Close your eyes. Visualize a stream of white and gold light entering your head through the crown chakra. Give it a name: the Universal Life Force, the Love of God, the Boundless Supply, whatever spontaneously comes to mind. This is your connection to all creation, to all wisdom, to all knowing. Allow the light to permeate the body. Send it through each of your chakras . . . the third eye . . . the throat . . . the heart . . . the solar plexus . . . the spleen . . . the root. Send it to all your body parts . . . your organs . . . your skin . . . your connective tissue . . . your muscle . . . your bones . . . your arteries and vessels . . . your nerves . . . your cells. Allow the light to flow out through your feet, into the ground . . . into the planet. You are now fully connected and grounded: open to the heavens above and planted in the earth below.

Quiet your thoughts as much as possible. The mind is busy, and even when we are relaxed, a continual mental chatter flows through us. The mind wants to wander. As thoughts arise let them go, like balloons drifting away on a wind, or water running through a sieve. The challenge is to not be distracted by thoughts and not get caught up in them. As you release your thoughts, gently sink deeper and deeper into a tranquil state of consciousness. Become a feather drifting downward through the air. When you come to rest, find profound peace.

Be present to the peace and stillness. Be filled with the white and gold light. Nothing more. When thoughts arise, let them go, softly, gently. Some days it takes longer to quiet the mind than others. No matter. You simply keep releasing. Do not try to stop your thoughts from originating—they are "mind waves," as they are called in Zen, and they pass.

If thoughts become particularly intrusive, recenter with the breath. Count the breath on the exhale up to fifteen. Start over again if necessary, and repeat as many times as necessary. Above all, stay relaxed. Some days are more productive for meditation than others. Do the best you can.

Stay in your meditative state for twenty minutes. If you are new to meditation, this may seem like a very long time. The more you meditate, however, the longer you will be able to sit and the deeper you will be able to go.

Return from your meditation by taking three deep breaths. Vigorously push the air out through the nose or mouth. Push energy out through your feet and feel the solid connection to earth. Feel firmly centered in your body. Open your eyes.

You may wish to spend some time journaling after meditation. Sometimes the intuitive flow stimulated by meditation appears later. Pay attention.

EXERCISE #2: OPEN-EYED MEDITATION

Most people naturally want to close their eyes for meditation. In Zen, however, one keeps them open. This is to remind us that we are part of the world around us, but detached from it. With eyes open, we are less likely to get sleepy and to produce daydreamlike mental imagery. And we are aware of what is going on in our environment, but we are not disturbed by it.

Try meditating with your eyes open. You will find it to be a much different meditational experience than with eyes closed. Perhaps you will even like it better!

Follow the steps in the Sitting Meditation. Instead of closing your eyes, keep them open and cast slightly downward, at about a forty-five-degree angle. Do not look at anything in particular. As in the Sitting Meditation, release thoughts and recenter as necessary. If activity enters your field of vision, treat it as you would thought and allow it to pass.

The zendo I once belonged to in Rye, New York, met in a Quaker church. The church was next door to the fire station. It was not unusual for our meditation to be punctured by blaring sirens and trucks screaming out of the garage. It was a wonderful discipline to maintain the still center with such distraction. Anyone can meditate in a quiet place. A true meditator can meditate anywhere, in the midst of commotion, and attain a state of enlightened consciousness.

EXERCISE #3: THE PEARL OF WISDOM MEDITATION

Jewels symbolize spiritual truths and wisdom, and the reflection of divine light. In myth and folk tale, a search for jewels represents a spiritual quest. To possess jewels is to possess knowledge and enlightenment.

In this exercise, we will work with the pearl, the special symbol of wisdom, as a doorway to the intuition. In esoteric lore, pearls represent the feminine principle, which in turn is associated with right-brain intuitive arts. Pearls once were sacred to the Mother Goddess. "Pearls of wisdom" were given out by Aphrodite Marina (Venus of the Sea) through her priestesses. As late as the Renaissance, it was believed that pearls were formed by an interaction between the sea and the moon, thus giving them strong associations with the lunar-governed forces of intuition, emotion, and the unconscious.

The pearl is also used in Zen as a symbol of perfection.

Follow the steps for Sitting Meditation. When you reach the still center, visualize a gleaming pearl hung in the black sea of space. Observe it carefully. Notice its color and glow, its smooth surface. Float around it in space, viewing the entire surface.

Merge with the pearl. Become one with the Pearl of Wisdom.

Using the breath, recenter in your body.

Make notes about your experience. What happened when you became one with the Pearl of Wisdom?

EXERCISE #4: THE JEWEL IN THE CROWN MEDITATION

This exercise is an advanced variation of the Pearl of Wisdom exercise. It is more active than the previous two exercises.

Instead of a pearl, we will work with the emerald. Jewels in a crown symbolize supreme wisdom. Our crown is of gold, the symbol of enlightenment.

The emerald is a powerful symbol in the Western mystery tradition. It represents all knowledge and Truth—everything that can be known but perhaps not expressed. Truth cannot always be put into words; it is experienced in the heart and intuited on a soul level.

The emerald has association with the Mother Goddess, especially in her vegetation aspect. Thus, it represents the renewal of the Earth and also immortality. In Biblical lore, the emerald was one of four stones given by God to Solomon.

The Holy Grail, the symbol of the mysteries of Christ and the illumined heart, is often described as an emerald or other jewel, as well as a cup or chalice.

The emerald also is a central image in the mystical path of Western alchemy. According to myth, Hermes Trismegistus ("Thrice greatest Hermes") was the greatest of all philosophers, the greatest of all kings, and the greatest of all priests. He is said to have reigned for 3226 years. He carried an emerald or emerald tablet upon which was recorded all of philosophy, knowledge, and the magical secrets of the universe.

Hermes Trismegistus is credited with writing forty-two sacred books (by some accounts many more) conveying the teachings of the gods. Most likely the books were authored between the third century B.C.E. and first century C.E.—or even later, well into the Middle Ages—by several anonymous persons in succession who signed them "Thoth" to give them weight and the appearance of antiquity.

This corpus, collectively known as the Hermetica, was housed in the great library in Alexandria. Most of them were lost when the library was burned by Christians. Surviving books were protected by a succession of initiates. Lore holds that the axiom of the Western mysteries, "That which is above is like that which is below," is inscribed on the Emerald Tablet. In other words, the realm of the gods is mirrored on Earth, and the external world is a reflection of the inner world. The axiom teaches that what we are on the inside—what we are spiritually—creates our material circumstances.

In dreams, emeralds often represent higher wisdom, especially if they are in the form of crown jewels or emerald eyes.

Gold symbolizes the sun, divine light, divine fire, illumination, the highest state of glory, and the Word of God or Truth. In alchemy, gold represents the attainment of the Philosopher's Stone, or enlightenment. It is the color of the masculine principle of the cosmos. Thus, in this exercise we have the masculine and feminine cosmic principles joined together over the third eye of intuitive and visionary sight.

Begin the Jewel in the Crown Meditation by following the steps for the Sitting Meditation. When you reach the still center, hold a vision of yourself radiant and filled with the white and gold light.

Allow yourself to become crowned with a beautiful band of gold. In the center of the crown is a large and brilliant emerald. Perhaps the crown simply appears on your head. Perhaps it descends from heaven. Perhaps it is given to you by an angel or spiritual being.

Observe your crown and stone. Is the crown simple or ornately carved? Are there symbols upon it? What is the cut of the gem? Feel the weight of the crown resting upon your forehead. Feel the radiance of the emerald. The energy of the crown and its jewel flow down the forehead to the third eye. The energy continues to flow down through the body, its emerald light mixing with the white and the gold.

Affirm to yourself silently, *I am illumined. I see Truth.*

Feel yourself permeated with the presence of Truth. Rest in this field of energy.

When you feel ready, recenter your consciousness with the breath and open your eyes.

Know that the Crown of Wisdom is part of you and that you always wear it.

Spend a few minutes journaling about your experience.

EXERCISE #5: THE CHALICE OF HIGHER WISDOM MEDITATION

In this exercise, we sit in the silence and become receptacles, or Holy Grails, to be filled with the Divine Mind. When we enter deep silence, we are inspired with fresh resolve, with new creative thought, with solutions to problems, and with the understandings of Truth that we need.

The Holy Grail legend has many stories associated with it. In Christianity, the grail represents the mystery of resurrection. The grail itself is a mystery, often described as a jeweled cup or chalice, or as a precious stone. In perhaps the best-known version of the legend, the grail is a cup that Joseph of Arimathea used to catch the blood of Christ as he was pierced with a spear while on the cross. After the crucifixion, Joseph took the grail to England and hid it in the area of Glastonbury.

In Arthurian lore, the grail symbolized the spiritual quest. At one Pentecost, the knights of King Arthur were gathered around the Round Table and a floating vision of the grail and the dove of the Holy Spirit appeared over them. The knights vowed to go in search of this grail. In their quest, they experienced obstacles, successes, and failures—just as we all do as we go through life.

The grail also is a symbol found universally in myth—that

of the cup of unending, eternal spiritual replenishment. When we drink from the grail, we take in the nourishment from the Source of All Being.

Follow the procedures for the Sitting Meditation. As you fill yourself with the white and gold light, visualize a luminous chalice within you. The chalice is centered in the heart. When the heart is illumined, we have found Truth; we are connected to divine Wisdom. Observe the chalice. What does it look like? Is it jeweled or inscribed? Is it on a tall stem or a short base?

Visualize and *feel* the white and gold radiance filling your chalice. There is no limit to how much your chalice can hold. Know that within the radiance is everything you need to know. It will reveal itself to you when the time is right.

Affirm to yourself silently, *My heart is illumined. I am filled with Truth.*

As the light continues to pour into your chalice, you are refreshed and revitalized. When you feel ready, recenter with the breath and open your eyes.

Know that the Chalice of Higher Wisdom is always within you. It is filled with an unlimited supply of spiritual wisdom, Truth, and nourishment.

EXERCISE #6: WALKING MEDITATION

Walking meditation is a refreshing change from sitting meditation. It moves spiritual energy through the body, which is important for nourishing the intuition.

Walking meditation can be done informally, such as a stroll through a garden or park or along the beach. It can be done as a walk through your neighborhood. It can also be done as a more formal ritual. However you choose to walk your meditation, it should be undertaken with *mindfulness*.

Prepare yourself for Walking Meditation by following the steps in Sitting Meditation for breathing and relaxing the body.

Fill yourself with the white and gold light and establish the connection to the heavens and the earth.

If you are walking informally, pace yourself slowly. Be aware of the connection of your feet to the ground. Use each of your senses to experience as much detail as possible around you. Try not to think of the past or the future; simply be present to the moment and the environment around you.

For a more formal Walking Meditation ritual, try the *kinhin* walking meditation of Zen. Once you are relaxed and centered and connected to the heavens and the earth, stand and take the *kinhin* walking posture. Make a loose fist with your left hand and place it over the solar plexus. Place your right hand over it in a gentle cup. This will push your elbows out from the body. Drop the shoulders to relax them. Keep the spine straight. Step forward with your right foot. Steps are taken very slowly, as though in slow motion. Your intent is to experience a deep contact with the Earth. Plant each foot and pause for a second or two, then slowly lift the foot and move forward. Keep your eyes cast downward at the forty-five-degree, half-mast angle.

Kinhin can be done indoors in a circumambulation around a room. The movement of the body brings new awareness that might have lain dormant while sitting.

Do a walking meditation at least once a week. One of my favorite variations is to do this indoors, with Gregorian chant music playing in the background. Gregorian chant is a body of more than three thousand works of sung psalms, hymns, and prayers. Composed in Latin, Gregorian chant flourished in monasteries during medieval times. It is a timeless style of music, calling to the monk in every soul. It brings one's total attention to the moment.

I begin with a period of Sitting Meditation and then do Walking Meditation. I finish with a short Sitting Meditation. I find that walking to Gregorian chant is especially consciousness-expanding in nature.

EXERCISE #7: THE GREAT SEAL MEDITATIONS

Buddhism teaches many ways to hold and poise the mind in meditation. Mahamudra ("Great Seal") meditation was practiced by the early Dalai Lamas of Tibet. Through it, one comes into an understanding of the true nature of the mind.

Mahamudra meditation is taught in metaphors. There are various mahamudra traditions; Buddha is credited with teaching the first. The following six pointers are common to most of the mahamudra traditions. Try them as a way of stilling the mind:

#1: *The mind should be kept like the sun in a cloudless sky.* The mind is like clear light, which is knowingness. Clouds represent wandering, distraction, torpor, and so on. When the clouds appear, let the sun disperse them gently so that they disappear.

#2: *The mind should be like an eagle soaring in the sky.* The eagle is graceful and powerful in the way it soars in flight with very little effort. Let the mind soar in luminous awareness.

#3: *The mind should be kept as the image of the ocean, deep and tranquil.* Disturbances—thoughts and phenomena—appear like ripples and waves on the surface. Let the mind become as the ocean when it appears as glass, smooth and calm.

#4: *The mind should be like a child in a temple.* A child has the ability to see an entire panorama and is open to the big view. Do not let the mind get bogged down by small details.

#5: *The mind should be like a bird in flight leaving no footprint.* The phenomena of the senses—heat and cold, pain, sound, rushes of energy, and so on—are like the footprints of the bird. They must be left behind in the flight of the mind.

Be not attached to phenomena. Allow them to arise and fall away.

#6: *The mind should be like a dandelion fluff in the autumn, picked up by the wind.* The mind should be kept light and buoyant. If the mind becomes heavy because of fatigue or the discomfort of the body, move the body slightly to restore the lightness.

You'll undoubtedly learn other meditation techniques besides the ones given here. Add those that work well for you to your repertoire. Keep your practice varied so that it doesn't become stale or predictable to you. Let meditation always be an adventure!

Chakra Energizing

LIKE KEY #1, INTUITIVE BREATHING, THIS EXERCISE IS ONE OF the basic essentials in your intuition training program. It will help you to:

- Become familiar with the chakras and their functions

- Stimulate the flow of the universal life force through your body and energy field

- Learn to experience your consciousness outside of your head, or thoughts

- Learn how to move your consciousness around

- Stimulate the intuitive faculty

Before you undertake this exercise, review the location and names of the chakras as described in chapter 2.

Sit in a comfortable chair, relaxed, with your spine straight. Relax with intuitive breathing.

Close your eyes and imagine yourself to be a ball of white light. All of your consciousness is centered in this light.

Move the light to the root chakra at the base of the spine. Feel the light pulsing there. Breathe into the light and into the root chakra for a minute or two.

Imagine that the light is on a string and you can pull it up. Pull the light into the second chakra, the spleen, located under the navel and to the left. Breathe into the light and the spleen chakra for a minute or two.

Then pull the light up into the third chakra, the solar plexus, located just below the navel. Feel the light pulsing there and breathe into the light and the chakra.

Continue on up the chakras, moving next to:

—the heart chakra in the center of the chest

—the throat chakra at the base of the throat

—the third eye chakra between and slightly above the brows

—the crown chakra at the top of the head

When you reach the crown, allow the light to cascade down around you so that you are enveloped in it. The seventh chakra is the seat of spiritual and mystical enlightenment and integration of our whole self.

AS YOU GO THROUGH THIS EXERCISE, YOU MAY NOTICE THAT it is difficult, perhaps even impossible, to leave certain chakras. If you feel resistance to pulling the light up, stay in the chakra. Visualize the light bathing the chakra in a soothing fashion. Move up only when you feel you can pull the light up. Your consciousness may be intuitively drawn to stay in a chakra because energy there needs to be stimulated.

Spend about twenty minutes on this exercise. If you only get through two or three chakras, that is fine. Pay attention to the intuitive impressions around each chakra.

For a variation on this exercise, change the color of the light to match each chakra:

Root—red

Spleen—orange

Solar plexus—yellow

Heart—green

Throat—blue

Third eye—indigo

Crown—violet

This exercise is also called chakra clearing. Energy in the chakras can become blocked or sluggish due to physical, emotional, and spiritual factors. Repressed emotions from our experiences can adversely affect the chakra energy as well. In esoteric thought, moving energy through them helps them to function better, and thus benefit our physical, mental, emotional, and spiritual health. When we're in optimum health, our intuition functions better, too.

Ball of Light

OUR INTUITION IS NONLOCAL IN THAT IT OPERATES INDEPEN-
dently of time and space. To give our intuition freer rein, we must
expand our experiences of our own consciousness.

When asked to pinpoint the location of consciousness, most
people say the head or the brain. We associate our thoughts and
feelings with the brain, and therefore what we are, our sum awareness, must be in the head.

In order to be intuitive, we have to get out of the head. We
must be comfortable with the idea that our consciousness is not
limited to the body. This is well demonstrated by the intuition
itself, which knows, sees, and understands things that are beyond
reach of the ordinary, body-contained senses.

Whether you are aware of it or not, your consciousness travels
all the time. It travels in the dreams of sleep, in the daydreams
of reverie, in flashes of insight or inspiration, in mutual moments
of "Oh, I was just thinking about you!"—and whenever the intuition functions.

The purpose of these exercises is to expand the boundaries of your self-awareness, the map you carry of the world of your consciousness. You can do them by yourself.

EXERCISE #1: TRAVELING AROUND THE BODY

Center yourself and relax with intuitive breathing.

Close your eyes and imagine yourself to be a ball of white light. All of your consciousness is centered in this light. Start with the light located in your head, where most of us identify the seat of consciousness. Fill your head with light. Feel its warmth. Spend a few minutes experiencing what it is like to be a ball of light inside the head. Perhaps you will see your brain lit from within.

Now move your light down into your heart. Feel your entire chest fill with light. What is it like to be centered in your heart?

Go down into your stomach. What do you see? What you do feel? Can you experience your own digestion? Do any thoughts or emotions arise from your stomach? If your stomach could talk, what would it tell you?

Move your light up into the throat. Spend a few minutes there, experiencing what the throat is, and what it has to tell you.

Move your light around your body. To your foot. Your hand. Various organs. The blood. Your bones.

Bring your light back to your heart. This is where your soul connection to the Source lies. To be intuitive, we must be heart-centered beings, not head-centered beings. The heart-centered person is open to exploration and is in touch with feelings and sensations. Allow your light to bathe and fill your heart. Send rays of light radiating out into the world. The rays of light are your consciousness and your soul essence, pouring forth in an eternal stream, connecting you to everything else in the cosmos. Feel the connection like links in a web. Everything is interwoven. You are part of the Web of All Things.

Recenter yourself in your body with intuitive breathing.

Record your experience in your journal.

EXERCISE #2: EXPANDING YOUR CONSCIOUSNESS

Center yourself and relax with intuitive breathing.

Close your eyes and imagine yourself to be a ball of white light. Place your light in the solar plexus chakra, just below the navel. The solar plexus, like the heart, maintains an important link to the Web of All Things for the intuition to travel on.

Feel your light fill the solar plexus. Experience its warmth.

Contract your light. Make it very small. The size of a baseball . . . a Ping-Pong ball . . . a pea. Make it infinitesimally small, so small the physical eye cannot see it. But the intuitive eye can.

Now make your light grow in size. It becomes bigger than a baseball. Allow it to keep growing. It extends beyond the solar plexus. It extends out from the body. Keep expanding the light until it becomes bigger than the body and envelopes the body in it.

Push the light out and out. Fill the room you are in. Move beyond the room. Fill the house or building you are in.

There are no limits to your light, just as there are no limits to your consciousness. You are the light. Keep expanding. Fill your city, your country, the planet. Extend into space. What do you experience?

Gradually contract your light. Recenter your consciousness in your body with intuitive breathing.

Record your experience in your journal.

EXERCISE #3: TRAVELING BEYOND THE BODY

Center yourself and relax with intuitive breathing.

Close your eyes and imagine yourself to be a ball of white light. Center your light comfortably within the body. Imagine that your light has become a balloon and can float upward. Float up to the ceiling in the room. Without looking at it with your physical eyes, "see" the detail of the ceiling and "feel" its texture. If this seems difficult, remind yourself that all of your senses have come with you in the light. It's perfectly natural and very easy for you to experience with your unlimited senses.

Now make your light grow heavy and descend to the floor. Again, without opening your physical eyes, see and feel the floor.

Bring your light up and move it around the room, keeping your eyes closed. Move into a corner. What do you experience? Look under a piece of furniture, cabinet, or table. What do you see?

Now move your light out of the room. Go into a hallway or adjacent room. Explore that area. Allow impressions to arise naturally. Do not worry about being accurate. Do not try to create impressions from memory of what you might know.

Return your light to your room and to your body. Recenter your light within your body with intuitive breathing.

Check the accuracy of your impressions.

Record your experience in your journal.

DO THESE EXERCISES FREQUENTLY. CHOOSE ONE EACH DAY for a week. They are building blocks for the more advanced exercises that follow in this book.

In Exercise 3, Traveling Beyond the Body, you can travel as far away as you want. However, it may then be impossible to verify the accuracy of your impressions. For best results, try places that you can easily visit to inspect later.

Expanded Vision

WHEN I HAVE VISITED JAPAN, I HAVE HAD THE PLEASURE OF attending tea ceremony classes taught by The Little Tea Society in Tokyo. My enjoyment of these classes led to further study of the history and ritual of tea. Japanese tea ceremony is both art form and spiritual path, and some of the fundamental elements in it pertain to the intuition.

In developing our intuition, we first learn to train our consciousness to hold a steady focus, and to expand our sensory awareness to pick up subtle and extrasensory cues and information. So it is with the tea ceremony. Everything in the ceremony is precise: the selection and arrangement of utensils; the arrangement and decorations of the tea room; the clothing worn; the order in which the ceremony is done. Server and participants have precise roles to play in what they do and say. All of this requires concentration and mindfulness. When you are doing tea, you are fully in the ceremony. Nothing else matters. The rest of the world recedes. Every bit of your attention and sensory awareness is focused.

The tea ceremony contains quite a bit of mystery to it. In fact, it is more than ceremony—it is *chado*, or "the way of tea."

Chanoyu, or the tea ceremony itself, arose in fifteenth-century Japan. It embodies the philosophy and rituals of Buddhism, Taoism, and Zen. Schools of tea arose and created tea masters who devoted their lives to perfecting the mystery of *chanoyu*. By practicing *chanoyu*, one unfolds spiritually.

In the tea ceremony, one pays careful attention to the senses. When the student enters the tea room, he devotes time to looking at it, appreciating its beauty. He listens to the sound of the water boiling in the tea kettle. He absorbs aromas and savors tastes. When the tea is served, he looks at the serving bowl, noticing its colors, texture, and artistry. He examines the tea utensils and containers. His careful observation enables him to see ordinary objects as extraordinary. It is a precious moment of eternity, never to be repeated.

In these exercises, we will focus our sense of sight as though we are students of tea. We will experience with the knowledge that we will never be in the same moment again. Thus, we will appreciate fully each moment.

EXERCISE #1: ZEN VIEWING

Go around your home and select five objects at random from any room. Five is the number of change, especially spiritual change. Thus it is the number of the intuition, for intuition brings change.

Arrange the objects in a row in front of you. Center yourself with intuitive breathing and relaxation. Contemplate your objects. Gaze at them one by one and as a group. One by one, pick up each object and give it your full attention. Observe colors, textures, imperfections, symmetry. Look at it as though you were seeing it for the first and last time in your life. Think about its origin and its purpose, who made it, its usefulness, and its place in your home. Record your impressions and thoughts for each object.

Do this exercise three times a week. What changes do you notice in how you look at things? Do you have a new and different appreciation of detail? Do you observe details that you did not before? Do you have a new and different appreciation about the objects themselves? How do these changes extend to the world beyond your home?

EXERCISE #2: APPRECIATING ART

Art is a manifestation of beauty, and when we contemplate beauty, we raise our spiritual consciousness and open the gateway to the intuition. Art is everywhere around us, of course, but museums and galleries offer us places to find concentrations of it. Yet how many times have you strolled through a museum and "looked" at the art as you walked by it?

In the East, appreciation of art is part of one's holistic spiritual path. Art speaks to the intuition in a direct way that bypasses words and linear thought.

Okakura Tenshin, who wrote the classic book about the Japanese tea ceremony, *The Book of Tea*, had this to say about the effect of art upon consciousness:

Nothing is more hallowing than the union of kindred spirits in art. At the moment of meeting, the art lover transcends himself. At once he is and is not. He catches a glimpse of Infinity, but words cannot voice his delight, for the eye has no tongue. Freed from the fetters of matter, his spirit moves in the rhythm of things. It is thus that art becomes akin to religion and ennobles mankind. It is this which makes a masterpiece sacred.[1]

For this exercise, visit a museum or art gallery. Select five works of art of any kind—painting, sculpture, pottery, artifact—

and study each one as you did with your home objects. You will not be able to touch or handle these, of course.

Immerse yourself in the minute details of each work. Contemplate its origin, purpose, and creator. If the artist is not known, allow your intuition to fill in the answer. What does each work of art have to say to you? What stories does it have to tell? Does it transport you to another time? What attracted you to this particular object?

The spirit, or consciousness, of the artist lives on in the work. Attune yourself to this spirit. What can your intuition tell you about the artist and his or her inspiration?

Record your experiences and thoughts.

EXERCISE #3: APPRECIATING GOD'S ART

Now we will turn our attention to the art gallery of nature. Choose a spot outdoors. It can be your backyard, a park, or a more exotic locale.

Prepare yourself as for meditation, with intuitive breathing and relaxation. Select five objects at random, near or distant: flowers, bushes, trees, stones, clouds, hills, or whatever draws your attention. It might also be an animal, such as a squirrel foraging for food.

Observe each in as much detail as possible, as though you are seeing it for the first and last time in your life. What drew you to your choices? What messages do they have for you? In the lore of angels, it is said that there is an angel to watch over everything in nature, including every blade of grass. Ask the angels of your choices to speak to you. Imagine a line of white and gold light extending from your heart to the heart of each thing you selected. Feel this connection. Now extend the connection to all of nature.

What do you experience? Record your thoughts and impressions.

*   *   *

ONE OF THE BENEFITS OF THESE EXERCISES — BESIDES strengthening the intuition—is to increase awareness of the indwelling spirit, or immanence, of God in all things. The divine spark is in everything in the world of nature, in all creatures, plants, stones, and geophysical features. The divine spark is manifest in whatever human beings create, including works of art and everyday objects intended to benefit daily life.

The awareness of this immanence makes the presence of God tangible. It puts us into direct contact with the power of creation. We not only see things differently, we see life differently. And we live life differently—more fully, more abundantly.

READING BODY LANGUAGE

Your expanded vision can be directed at the body language signals given by others. Our bodies express what we're *really* feeling or thinking. Intuitives pay attention to detail, and detail reveals a great deal of information. There are obvious body language signals that most of us know. For example, crossed arms and/or legs often indicate defensiveness. Many body language signals are subtle. When you talk to others, listen with your eyes as well as your ears. What is communicated to you intuitively? How well does body language match what is being said?

You may want to study the literature on body language, but do not allow it to set preconceived ideas for you. Be open to what the intuition has to tell you from your observations.

Expanded Listening

THE SKILLED INTUITIVE LEARNS TO HEAR WITH THE INNER ear as well as the outer ear. In these exercises, we will extend our physical sense of hearing to pick up on the subtle sounds and cues of the world around us and on the inner plane.

The practice of Expanded Listening will help you to develop an entirely new sense of hearing. Mystics experience this spiritual, or soul, hearing. According to Rudolph Steiner, all higher truths are obtained only through the disciplined use of senses to experience inner promptings:

> The soul becomes capable of hearing "words" from the spiritual world that are not expressed in outer tones and cannot be heard by physical ears. Perception of the "inner world" awakens. Truths are gradually revealed to us out of the spiritual world. We hear ourselves spoken to spiritually.[1]

Intuition flows from the higher truths or Truth.

EXERCISE #1: SOUNDS OF THE OUTER ENVIRONMENT

In your own home, settle into a comfortable spot and enter a meditative state with your eyes closed. Allow the silence to thicken around you. Listen to the sounds of the environment around you: cars passing by on the street, airplanes flying overhead, birds singing outside, appliances humming, and so on. Experience each sound fully. Allow it to pass through you.

Now imagine that your ears are extremely sensitive antennae. Extend your listening out farther and farther into physical space. Can you hear the sounds of a highway some distance away? The sound of an appliance in another part of the house? The sounds of the airport twenty miles away? The sound of a river one hundred miles away? The sound of the ocean two hundred miles away? The sounds of a city one thousand miles away? And so on. Keep pushing out the boundaries of what you can hear. There are no limits. Become immersed in the sounds.

After you end the exercise, record your experiences.

As a variation, you can start this exercise out-of-doors and focus on the sounds of nature. Hear the obvious sounds. Then, as you extend your sensitivity, listen for the softer and more subtle sounds of nature: the rustling of small animals and birds in bushes, leaves rustling in trees, insects crawling through blades of grass, the sound of clouds moving through the sky, the sound of things growing.

Record your experiences.

EXERCISE #2: SOUNDS OF THE INNER ENVIRONMENT

Enter into a meditative state with your eyes closed. Become aware of the sounds of your environment. Allow them to pass through you.

Now turn your attention inward. Listen carefully to the sound of your breathing. Become totally immersed in the sound.

Go deeper. Hear your heartbeat. Listen to your digestion. Then go deeper still to hear the blood rushing through the veins and arteries. Go deeper still. Hear the sounds of cells doing their jobs to keep your physical house functioning. Listen for the impulses of brain activity.

Go deeper still, deep into the interior of your being, where you hear the sound of the cosmic currents of being.

Record your experiences. Did any sounds surprise you?

THE INTUITION OFTEN SPEAKS THROUGH SUBTLE ENVIRON-mental cues. Do these exercises often to sharpen your listening skills. Affirm to yourself, "*I hear Truth.*"

Make note of any other intuitive information that comes as a result of expanded listening: messages, information, ideas, and so on.

The more you develop your inner hearing, the more selective you will become about what you hear. Background sound and noise that once seemed necessary to you—such as a radio or television set going constantly—will become less desirable. Discordant sound and the sound of violence—such as that present in much popular music, film, and TV shows—will also become less desirable. You will find yourself naturally preferring silence or sounds that are pleasing and harmonious.

Perhaps one of your experiences of Expanded Listening was to hear the sound of creation. Primordial sound, as it is called in mystical traditions, is sound beyond sound. From primordial sound come the sounds of divinity as expressed in all the names of God.

Our spiritual health—and therefore our intuitive health—is governed by the diet we feed it. Our diet consists of not only the food we eat, but also what we eat with our ears and our eyes.

Riding the Waves

ALL THINGS IN THE UNIVERSE ARE COMPOSED OF ENERGY. The energy can assume any form, and can become organized into patterns, such as the physical realm. Matter is energy. Consciousness is energy. Our thoughts and feelings are energy. Creativity is energy. Intuition is energy. The essence of the soul is energy.

The energies of the universe are in constant motion and interplay. As energies affect one another, they change form. In this exercise, we will change the form of our energy, transmuting the body, which has limitations, into waves of energy, which have no limit. As a wave of energy, you can travel wherever you need to go to tap into your intuition.

EXERCISE #1: RIDING THE WAVES

Imagine yourself at the seashore. Stand with bare feet at the water's edge. Watch the waves roll in and lap at the beach. Smell the salt air. Feel the crunch of the sand beneath your feet. Hear the sound of the waves, the cries of shore birds. The ocean stretches into infinity.

Notice that the sunlight falling upon the water makes the surface sparkle like millions of gems. You are warm, happy, and content. You are fully present in the moment. There is no past, no tomorrow, only the eternal moment.

Focus your attention on the action of the waves. The water rolls in, the water rolls out. Timeless, eternal motion.

Imagine that your consciousness flows out from you in waves of energy. See the waves rippling from you. Synchronize the waves of your consciousness with the ocean waves. Let yourself become lighter and lighter. Your body begins to change into waves of energy. Become lighter still, until you are only energy. Flow out over the ocean waves.

Now you are a wave of energy riding along the waves of the ocean. Feel the flow, the surge and ebb. The tide is going out. Allow yourself to be carried along with it, easily, gently. You are filled with complete peace and harmony, at one with the sparkling ocean. You feel energized. The ocean is the universe. You are one with the currents of the universe.

The currents carry you out and out. Here you are free of distraction. Here you are free of limitation. You can know the answers to all questions. You can know all things.

A message is given to you. Perhaps the ocean speaks it. Perhaps a bird cries it. Perhaps the clouds write it across the sky. Perhaps it wells up within you as something you knew all along.

Give thanks for your message. Know that it is right for you.

When you feel ready, return to awareness of your physical body.

Record your experience. What impressions did you have of what "you" were like in form?

Riding the Waves will help you become comfortable with operation of your intuition as an ability not limited by your body.

Remote Viewing

In Expanded Vision (Key #5), we learned to focus our vision on detail and subtle cues. Now we will work with our inner vision and send it to hidden and distant locations. The modern term for this is "remote viewing." It is a psychic/intuitive skill known and used since ancient times. In the past, it has been called "traveling clairvoyance" and "telesthesia." The term "remote viewing" was coined in the 1970s by American physicists Russell Targ and Harold Puthoff, who researched the phenomenon. Targ also called it "remote sensing," since impressions of smell, sound, and touch are part of the experience.

Historically, remote viewing has been associated with psychically gifted and trained persons such as oracles, shamans and magical adepts and mediums. The faculty of remote viewing is one of the *siddhis* described in the *Yoga Sutras* written by Patanjali about three thousand years ago. The *siddhis* are paranormal or extraordinary powers attained through spiritual development, such as through various paths of yoga. *Siddhis* means "perfect abilities" or "miraculous powers." They include clairvoyance (the ability to see distant places and things), telepathy, mind reading, levitation, materialization, invisibility, superhuman strength, knowledge of one's death, and the ability to project out of one's own body and into another's body. The *siddhis* should not be sought for themselves. Rather, they arise as a natural part of spiritual advancement. If one gets caught up in their enchantment, one stops spiritual advancement.

In the late eighteenth and early nineteenth centuries, hypnotists observed that ordinary people, when hypnotized, often could give detailed accounts of distant locations. Not only could they describe surroundings, people, clothing, and activities, some could "see" into distant stomachs to report their contents, and "see" into brains. Meanwhile, mediums popularized public performances of "billet reading," in which they "read" messages in sealed envelopes with eyes closed or while blindfolded. Psychical researchers conducted many controlled scientific experiments with blindfolded subjects.

Targ and Putoff, using more sophisticated modern methodologies, collected impressive results in their experiments with remote viewing (they established a research project at SRI International, formerly Stanford Research Institute). They concluded that remote viewing is a psychic experience that occurs naturally in the lives of many people. They found they could train others to remote view, regardless of their natural psychic ability and previous psychic experiences or training. Most remote viewers can be taught to go to a location and accurately describe buildings, geographic features, people, and activities. In many cases, the farther away the target, the greater the accuracy. They also can be taught to see into opaque containers to describe contents (the modern version of billet reading), and to read data and see images on microdot film. The U.S. government became interested and financed research into the possible uses of remote viewing for intelligence gathering, warfare, and espionage. Viewers were given intensive training. Typically, they were asked to describe distant locations knowing only the latitude and longitude as reference points. Overall, the government's success in psychic espionage was mixed, perhaps for reasons elaborated below.

Once rather exotic, remote viewing classes and training are now readily available to the general public. There's nothing difficult or tricky about it—anyone can learn to send his consciousness traveling to a distant or physically inaccessible spot. With training and practice come increasing accuracy.

Remote viewing has various practical applications. Remote viewers are used to survey distant sites. They are flown over terrain to sense hidden water sources and mineral, gem, coal, and gas deposits. Psychics who work with police on crime solving use remote viewing to try to locate missing persons or bodies. Remote viewing can look into the past to re-create a crime victim's last activities and movements. Looking into the past (also called retrocognition) may be of use in archaeology. Remote viewing can also look into the future. Several of the Keys in this section utilize remote viewing in different ways.

A word about ethics: Some people are drawn to remote viewing training because they think it will enable them to spy upon others. In the mystical traditions, the misuse of the power of the *siddhis* boomerangs back upon the user, ultimately affecting overall health. Remote viewers have found that people who do not wish their privacy of place or person invaded will not be open to invasion. And, they find that the continued use of remote viewing for selfish purposes drains one's vitality. The higher powers respond to higher spiritual laws. When you undertake remote viewing, it must be for the purposes of help and healing, not for entertainment.

EXERCISE #1: PLACE VIEWING

For this exercise, you will need a partner. Decide who will be the tester and who will be the subject. In advance, the tester will select five images of places and place them inside opaque, sealed envelopes. The images can be photos, drawings, or pictures clipped from magazines. They could be of cityscapes, nature vistas, buildings, and so on. They must be *places*. Number the envelopes and make a record of the contents of each.

Arrange a time to get together with your partner, the subject. Place sealed envelope #1 in front of the subject. The subject has fifteen minutes to "see" the image inside. The subject should write down his or her impressions, including any drawings. The subject is not allowed to handle the envelope.

When the first envelope is done, continue through the remaining four, one by one. At the completion, open the envelopes one by one and see how well the subject did.

The subject's impressions may be generalized. For example, you may see geometric impressions and not specific landscape features. Straight lines may be tall buildings.

Do this exercise regularly, switching roles and shortening the time the subject has to receive and record impressions to five minutes. Are you more accurate with less time? Sometimes, the more time we have to think about our impressions, the less accurate we are because we make judgments on what we receive.

EXERCISE #2: PEOPLE VIEWING

Make arrangements with a friend or family member that you will look in on them by remote viewing at an appointed time. Select a time during which the other party—henceforth your target—knows where he will be. For example, at 8 P.M., he will be at home. At 10 A.M., he will be in the office. These are places with which you should have at least some familiarity: you have seen the home, and know at least something general about the office (such as its location downtown, for example). Ascertain only the place where the target will be; do not collect any information about what your target will be doing.

Prepare yourself as for meditation with intuitive breathing

and relaxation. Close your eyes. Think of the target and call up a vivid visual impression and name. Visualize them where they are in as much detail as possible. At first this will seem like an exercise of imagination, but your expanded senses will take over quickly.

Release any expectations you have of what the target *should* be doing. You must be open and neutral to whatever impressions arise. Pretend you are watching a movie—you don't know what's going to happen next. Do not judge or analyze any impressions, which will immediately interfere with the process. For example, if a piece of furniture seems out of place, do not question its location—it may in fact have been moved.

Can you picture your target clearly? What is he doing? What details in the surroundings do you notice? Do you receive any emotional impressions? Do you notice any sounds or smells? Do you feel any sensations of heat or cold? Are there other people in your remote viewing movie?

Record your impressions, no matter how sketchy. You may not experience anything like a movie, but instead receive fragments of impressions. Do not disregard anything.

Later, check with your target. How well do your impressions match what really transpired?

Do this beginning exercise several times. The more you practice it, the better results you will obtain. You will notice more detail.

Variations of remote viewing are presented in Key #17, Hide-and-Seek.

Reading Objects and Photographs

EVERYDAY OBJECTS ARE REPOSITORIES OF INFORMATION AC-cessible by intuition and psychic skill. Sound impossible? It's an age-old, worldwide belief, one that has been borne out by experience. Obtaining information from objects is called psychometry, from the Greek words *psyche* (the soul) and *metron* (measure). There is no scientific basis for psychometry, but I can assure you that it works. I have used psychometry for years. And now is your chance to test out your own psychometry ability. Consider it your "expanded touch."

The idea behind psychometry is that objects retain an energy imprint of people who own them and handle them over a period of time. If an intuitive person holds the object and "tunes in," impressions about the owner(s) will arise. Whether or not any actual "vibrations" are imprinted upon an object will perhaps forever be a matter of conjecture. The bottom line is that psychometry seems to open intuitive/psychic doorways. The objects may be nothing more than props, but, like other intuitive tools, they facilitate the flow of intuitive information. You've probably seen psychics at work, perhaps on television or in a reading being done for you, who ask to hold clothing, jewelry, personal items, and so on. They are using psychometry.

There's an interesting history to psychometry. The word was coined in 1840, by Joseph R. Buchanan, an American professor of physiology who saw psychometry as a means to measure the "soul" of objects and "grasp and estimate all things which are within range of human intelligence." Buchanan conducted experiments in which students could identify drugs in vials by holding the vials. He kept his research quiet for nine years out of fear of ridicule.

Buchanan's work interested Professor William F. Denton, an American professor of geology, who conducted his own experiments in 1854, with his sister, Ann Denton Cridge. When Cridge placed wrapped geological specimens to her forehead, she experienced vivid mental images of their appearances. Denton, who did not consider the possibility of telepathy between himself and his sister, recorded his experiments in a book, *The Soul of Things*. He defined psychometry as a "mysterious faculty which belongs to the soul and is not dependent upon the body for its exercise."

Psychometry was popularized by mediums, who "read" the contents of sealed letters. Today, psychometry is used in psychic criminology and psychic archaeology. In psychic criminology, psychics handle a personal object belonging to or associated with a crime victim or missing person in order to get clues that will help solve the crime or locate the person or body. Objects worn during stress, especially the trauma of crime, convey the most vivid impressions. In psychic archaeology, psychics receive impressions from artifacts to identify their uses and historical dates. Even stones and bricks yield data.

Every intuitive finds the methods that work best for him or her. Years ago, I began to use psychometry and continue to use it today. When I hold someone's watch or ring, I receive intuitive impressions in the form of images, words, and feelings.

Everyone interested in intuitive development should try psychometry. You'll probably be surprised at what you can do!

EXERCISE #1: READING OBJECTS

For this exercise, work with a partner, ideally someone you do not know well or at all. You will need a small personal possession and notepad and pen. Preferably, your possession should be made of metal, as metal seems to retain the strongest impressions. Jewelry, watches, cosmetics cases, keys, and keychains all can do quite nicely. For best results, the object should belong only to the wearer and should have been in possession for at least three months. Gifts from others are fine, but avoid such things as antique or secondhand jewelry, or jewelry handed down through families. The objects will have the energy imprints of all their owners, and thus you will receive confusing or muddy intuitive impressions.

Exchange objects with your partner. Each of you close your eyes and hold the object. Pay attention to the spontaneous words, images, and thoughts that arise to your inner mind and eye. Do not disregard or discard anything, no matter how incongruous or "inappropriate" it seems. Do not evaluate or judge! Just pay attention.

Intuitively examine your object for five minutes without speaking. Look at it also with open eyes. Jot down notes about your impressions and any associations with them, so that you don't forget anything. You may be flooded with impressions. Or, you may receive one or two. Don't be frustrated if you receive very little—sometimes a single, small impression unlocks a wealth of insight. Don't try to force more. Your expectation, fear of failure, and imagination will interfere.

When the five minutes is up, take turns sharing your impressions. Do not provide any feedback until the other person is done speaking about you. If you don't know what an impression means, just say so. Most likely, you will have an intuitive feel for what an impression conveys.

For example, once in a reading for a young man, I had a vivid image of a horse racetrack while I held his watch. The empty track was muddy and pounded, as though many horses had gone over it. What could that mean? Did he like to go to the races? Did he own a racehorse? Was he in a race against time? The intuitive feeling that accompanied this image said otherwise. I felt that he was stressed by competition. He wasn't one of the horses or jockeys, however (note that my impression featured neither of those). He was the racetrack, and that's how he felt—pounded. Furthermore, I had the feeling that this did not relate to work (the logical assumption), but to family. All of these impressions and more arose simultaneously in my mind while I held the watch.

I described the image to him and said, "I have the feeling that you experience a lot of competition for attention in your family, and that you're in a race to be the first or the best. This is the way it's always been, and you're tired of it. It has drained a lot of your energy, especially your emotional energy, and it's not getting you anywhere—you just keep going around in circles. It's somebody else's race, not yours. Deep inside, you'd like to quit it."

It was all right on target. The young man was struggling with a desire to pursue his own interests in life rather than fulfill the expectations of a competitive family. The image of the empty and pounded track was a powerful one for him, validating his true feelings.

Another time, as I held a woman's ring, I saw a tennis ball bouncing back and forth across a net. No players or racquets, just a ball going from this side to that. It turned out that the woman was in the middle of a family dispute and was being bounced from one side to the other. The dispute was more a "game" between two family members who were both using her. She was able to extricate herself from the situation without guilt.

Not all impressions are going to deal with major matters. For example, you may see an image of a house filled with vases of lovely flowers, and then learn that your partner loves to garden and keeps her house filled with cut blossoms.

Try a new partner. This time, hold the objects for one minute instead of five. Then describe your impressions and associations.

Try another new partner. You will not need your notepads or pens, but will work alternately, one at a time. Take your partner's object, hold it, and begin speaking immediately. When you are done, let your partner give feedback. Switch roles.

This progression of faster and faster responses will help you train your intuitive awareness to be rapid and fluid. Also, you will not have time to stop and evaluate what you are receiving, so you are less likely to let left-brain judgment interfere. Intuition arises quickly.

EXCERCISE #2: READING HIDDEN OBJECTS

For more challenge, wrap your object in a bit of tissue and seal it inside a plain white envelope. In the exercise, handle only the sealed envelope. You may or may not be able to guess what the object is—it doesn't matter—but you will not have unconscious associations that can arise from seeing it, such as "This is an expensive watch, so he must be affluent," or "This is an odd ring, so she must like unusual things."

Follow the procedures outlined in Exercise 1.

EXERCISE #3: READING PHOTOGRAPHS

Is a photograph a lifeless image, or does it contain a spark of a person's essence, soul, or spirit? Many peoples around the world believe that it does, and therefore do not like to have their photos taken, especially by strangers.

There's some truth in that belief. A photograph may not steal your soul, but it does carry your essence, and can be psychometrized like your personal possessions and your aura. Now that you have gained some familiarity with psychometry, try your skill on photographs.

Select two photos from your personal collection: one of you and one of a family member or friend who is living. For best results, the photos should be recent. Current information can be obtained from old photographs, but may be obscured by old information.

Work with a partner who also has selected two photographs. Neither of you shares any information about the photos, when or where they were taken, or the identities of the other persons. Exchange the photos of yourselves. Spend three minutes examining them and recording your impressions. Try to see beyond the photos themselves. Experiment with averted vision. Hold the palm of one hand over the photo. Don't be surprised if the photo seems to come "alive." Perhaps the image will talk to you intuitively. Perhaps you will see objects or places in the space around the photograph. You may receive impressions of emotions, or of events that have happened to the person.

When the time is up, set those photos aside and take the second photos. Do the same, spending three minutes reading them and recording your impressions.

When the reading period is finished, share your intuitive impressions about both photographs. Wait for your partner to give all impressions on both photos before offering any feedback.

How did you do? Were you able to correctly identify the second person? Or perhaps you saw something, such as an activity, that linked that person to your partner. Were your impressions predominantly emotional in tone? Or did you see mostly events?

A mixture? Were any of your impressions precognitive, relating to possible future events?

How did you feel about photographs compared to your psychometry practice with objects?

IF YOU DON'T FEEL IN THE FLOW AFTER REPEATED PRACTICE with psychometry, don't worry. It doesn't mean you are not intuitive. Everyone has his or her resonances with different intuitive techniques.

Reading Auras

BESIDES OBJECTS, A PERSON'S AURA CAN BE PSYCHOME-
trized. To a clairvoyant, the envelope of energy around someone
contains a wealth of physical, mental, emotional, and spiritual
information about them.

But you don't have to be a born clairvoyant or a professional
psychic in order to read the aura. Whether you're aware of it or
not, you are reading the aura whenever you meet someone. We
all have first impressions that we cannot ascribe to known facts.
People make us feel at ease or ill at ease; we sense sadness around
them even when their demeanor is happy, and so on.

This exercise is similar to psychometry with objects; familiarize yourself with Key #9 first.

EXERCISE #1: READING AURAS WITH TOUCH

On straight-backed chairs, sit facing a partner. You can also
sit on the floor if you like, but make sure that both of you can be
comfortable for some time. Sitting cross-legged on the floor is not
easy for everyone. Decide which of you will read first.

Relax and center with intuitive breathing. Imagine that the two of you are enveloped in a bubble of white light. The white light wraps you in a loving energy. Send loving thoughts to your partner, wishing that whatever comes from the exercise will be of benefit to him.

When you feel ready, hold out your hands palms up. Your partner will place his or her hands palm down on top of yours. Through this connection, you are tapped in to the energy of your partner's aura. Allow your intuitive impressions to arise spontaneously within you. You can keep your eyes closed or open. You are likely to feel more comfortable with them closed. Allow your mind to float and stay detached from results.

Hold the connection for three minutes. You can rest your hands on your lap. When the time is up, thank your partner and share your impressions. Receive feedback. Then switch roles.

Like the Objects exercise, this one also progresses in speed. Change partners and do it again, spending only one minute tuning in through the hands, then share your impressions and get feedback. Switch roles.

Change partners again, and this time begin speaking as soon as you connect through the hands.

THE FIRST TIMES YOU TRY THIS EXERCISE, YOU MAY FREEZE UP under the pressure of performing in a short period of time. Relax and keep trying. Remember that the more relaxed you are, the more successful you will be. Don't be concerned about how much intuitive material you can produce. None of these exercises is a contest. Trust that you will receive what will be of help to your partner. That may be a lot, or it may be a single impression.

EXERCISE #2: READING AURAS WITHOUT TOUCH

Try this series again, but without any physical contact with your partner. Sit facing him or her. Imagine the white bubble of loving energy around the two of you, send loving thoughts, and ask to be of help. Then allow your impressions to arise.

Did you notice a difference in using touch versus not touching? Was one method more productive for you? For some, even a slight contact facilitates the flow of impressions, rather like holding a metal object.

Even if you felt you got more from touching, practice this exercise frequently without touch. In real-life application, it is not always feasible—or advisable—to touch others. These different techniques will teach you the subtleties of your own intuition. Ultimately, you will feel confident about tapping into your intuition anytime and anywhere.

Pendulum Dowsing

THE PENDULUM IS A POPULAR TOOL FOR ACTIVATING THE IN-tuitive/psychic sense. It has been used for thousands of years in dowsing, which is a form of divination for locating lost and missing persons and animals, and for detecting hidden objects and substances, such as water, oil, coal, minerals, cables, and pipes. Dowsing is also used in the mapping of archaeological sites. Many people dowse as a way of asking the intuition about decisions and choices for virtually any purpose.

No one knows exactly how or why dowsing works. The tool responds to the user. For example, if a dowser is looking for underground water with rods, the rods will signal where the water is by moving up and down or back and forth. A pendulum will begin to whirl. Along with the signals from the tool, the dowser may also get intuitive visual impressions. Dowsers do not necessarily need to go on location to search for things. Many dowse maps in a type of remote viewing.

Dowsing is at least seven thousand years old; its exact origins are unknown. Rods of wood or metal (even coat hangers) are used as well as pendula. Ancient Egyptian art portrays dowsers with forked rods and headdresses with antennae. Ancient Chinese kings used dowsing rods. The Kalahari bushmen of Africa have long used dowsing to find sources of water.

During the Middle Ages, dowsing was used widely in Europe and Great Britain to locate underground water and coal deposits. It was associated with the supernatural, which gave rise to the terms "water witching" and "wizard's rod." Among the first books on the subject were *The Diviners* by Gaspard Peucer, published in 1553, and *De Re Metallica* by Agricola, published in 1556, in Germany. Dowsing was transplanted to America by the early colonists.

Dowsing was widely used until the nineteenth century, when scientists dismissed it as superstition. In the twentieth century, dowsing made a comeback as an intuitive skill, especially in Europe and Great Britain, where it has been successfully used in archaeological digs, the search for minerals, and in medicine. During war time, dowsers helped locate mines, unexploded shells, and buried bombs for the military.

In the United States, dowsing is used by some oil, gas, and mineral companies, who have found dowsers to be often more accurate than geologists using "scientific" techniques. Many water and pipe companies use dowsing to locate buried cables and pipes find damaged spots. In the Vietnam War, the Marines used dowsing rods to locate mines, booby traps, and sunken mortar shells. Dowsers also have contributed research toward the understanding of mysterious earth energies, such as ley lines.

The pendulum has become the dowsing tool of choice over rods, perhaps due to its small size and convenience. It can be easily kept in a pocket or pouch. Some pendula can be quite fancy and expensive, made out of sterling silver chains and carved crystals or precious stones. Others are less elegant and costly, but are equally effective. The pendulum is simply a tool for focusing your intuition.

Whether you buy a pendulum or make one yourself, here are

some ideal specifications from professional dowsers to keep in mind:

The pendulum should be onion or pear shaped, symmetrical about its vertical axis and about two and one-half to three inches at the largest diameter. It can be solid or hollow with a screw top. Another form of pendulum is cylindrical with two conical ends and about three to five inches long. The weight should be about fifty grams. Dowsers who work primarily indoors with documents can have a lighter weight from fifteen to thirty grams. Pendula for outdoor work are heavier, up to one hundred and fifty grams.

The pendulum hangs from a cord, which may be of thread, an anti-twist nylon, or a chain.

The cord should be held between the thumb and forefinger of either hand with up to about eight inches of cord between the thumb and the pendulum. Most dowsers determine their own ideal length of cord according to their experience.

FOR THESE EXERCISES YOU WILL NEED TO BUY OR MAKE YOUR own pendulum. Many esoteric bookstores sell them. Some people find that any kind of weight suspended on a string works very well for them. If you make a pendulum, be sure that the object hangs straight when suspended by your fingers.

EXERCISE #1: TRAINING THE PENDULUM

First you must train the pendulum to say yes and no. Center yourself with intuitive breathing to achieve a relaxed and tranquil mind. Hold the pendulum steady and ask, "Give me a yes." Do not try to stimulate movement. Allow it to respond naturally. After a few moments, the pendulum will begin to rotate or swing back and forth. The more vigorous the motion, the stronger the response. Stop the pendulum and hold it steady again. Ask, "Give me a no." Allow the pendulum to respond naturally again.

Most likely, the no will be the opposite motion of the yes. If the pendulum rotates clockwise for yes, it probably will rotate counterclockwise for no (rather than swing back and forth, for example).

Ask the pendulum a series of yes and no questions to which you know the answers. "Is my name John Doe?" "Do I live at 47 Jackson Street?" and so on. With each question, allow the pendulum to respond of its own accord. If it remains motionless, ask the question again.

Then ask questions that have emotional intensity behind them—something you feel strongly about that can be worded in a yes or no way. Does your pendulum respond more vigorously?

Work with your pendulum every day by asking it obvious questions. Trust the pendulum to reflect your intuition.

EXERCISE #2: YES AND NO

Once you feel comfortable working with your pendulum, use it daily to pose yes or no questions. Start with simple things, such as a route to work, an activity, an errand, etc. If you start with major issues, you may be nervous about the results and have difficulty opening your intuition.

If you ask a question and the pendulum does not respond, it may mean neutrality.

When you feel secure in trusting the response of the pendulum, gradually increase the importance of questions you pose.

You can also consult the pendulum for timing. Keep in mind that questions need to be framed in a yes-or-no context. For example, if you are contemplating a move, you can ask questions like "Would spring be a good time to move?" or "Would next month be a good time to move?"

Look for ways to validate the answers. Perhaps something worked out well in your favor, or you avoided an inconvenience. Notice any corresponding intuitive signals from your body, senses, or impressions that arise in the mind.

EXERCISE #3: LOST AND FOUND

For this exercise, you will need a partner. One of you will hide an object; the other will find it with pendulum dowsing.

First, an object known to both parties will be hidden indoors, such as in a person's home. The seeker will search for it with the pendulum.

Visualize the object as vividly as possible in your mind. Give verbal instructions to the pendulum to alert you to its location. Hold the pendulum steady and then walk around the site. When the pendulum starts to move in an affirmative manner, such as swinging in clockwise circles, you know you are close. The closer you are, the more the pendulum should move.

Try this exercise out of doors.

In a more difficult variation, an object unknown to the seeker is hidden indoors. You, the seeker, cannot visualize it, but you can ask the pendulum to locate the hidden object and reveal its identity. Follow the movements of the pendulum. The closer you are, the more the pendulum will move. The object may be truly hidden from sight, or may be in plain view.

Do this variation of the exercise out of doors.

In all cases, note how long it takes you to locate the target object. What special clues or feelings do you associate with a hit? What clues did you ignore?

EXERCISE #4: PLACE IDENTIFICATION

For this exercise, you will need photographs of places and maps that include their sites. The photographs should be of places that are not readily identifiable, but can be pinpointed on a map. The maps can be of a region, country, or the world. For example, you might have a photograph of a house in a city.

The subject, or dowser, is shown a photo of a place. He or she is given a map and asked to identify the location of the place with the pendulum.

Hold the pendulum still over the map. Slowly move it over the surface. Follow the actions of the pendulum. When you come close to the location, the pendulum should react with movement. Follow your intuition to what you feel is the strongest movement.

How accurate are you? Do you identify the precise location (such as a city) or do you come close (geographic region)?

IF YOU RESONATE STRONGLY WITH THE PENDULUM, YOU ARE likely to make it your constant companion. I know people who use a pendulum to help them make decisions at work—though they would never admit so to their superiors!

The Dream Oracle

OUR INTUITION SPEAKS TO US CONSTANTLY THROUGH OUR dreams, helping us solve problems and obtain guidance. The importance of dreams as a direct line to higher wisdom has been recognized since ancient times. In these exercises, you will learn how to program your dreams for answers to questions, how to send and receive messages in dreams, and how to use dreams to look into the future.

EXERCISE #1: INCUBATION

People around the world have practiced ways to ask questions specifically for answers in dreams. These ways are called dream incubation, from the Greek term *incubatio,* or "sleeping in." We incubate dreams by impressing and holding a request for information within consciousness, so that a desired dream is born into our awareness.

The ancients had special places where one went to seek help from the gods through dreams. These were sacred caves, groves, or temples. In the classical world, there were once more than four

hundred temples devoted to the Greek god of healing, Aescula-
pius. Pilgrims would undertake special trips to a temple. Upon
arrival, they would prepare themselves with rituals of fasting,
cleansing, sacrifice, and prayer. They would go to sleep hoping
that the god or one of his totem animals would come to them in
their dreams and either heal them or tell them how they could be
healed.

We can do dream incubation today right in the sacred temple
of our own home. We do not have to remove ourselves to the
wilderness to tap into this intuitive resource.

Treat dream incubation as a ritual. A ritual is a set of inten-
tions and actions that changes consciousness, thus opening the
channels for the Higher Self to speak. The procedure here engages
the senses, which heightens the opening of the intuitive channels.

In general, it's a good idea to eat lightly the day (and especially the evening) of your incubation. Many old incubation techniques call for fasting, which isn't essential, but a matter of
personal preference. Avoid heavy food and alcohol, which can disrupt the sleep cycle.

At the start of the day, frame your question. Make it simple
and clear: "Should I take the new job offer in Chicago?" The
simpler your question, the easier it will be to understand your
dream's answer. By framing your question early in the day, it will
be cooking away in the back of your mind until bedtime. Write
the question down in your journal. Think about the question
often, followed by an affirmation: "Should I take the new job offer
in Chicago? *My dreams will tell me the answer tonight.*"

Prior to bedtime, relax with a little inspirational reading.
Lighting a candle or burning incense adds to the sensory pleasure
of the ritual, thus heightening your anticipation. Turn your attention to your incubation question. Write it down again. You
may want to write it on notepaper and place it beneath your pillow
(thus you would literally "sleep on it"!). Hold question and affirmation strongly in your mind. Repeat it silently or out loud three

times. You may wish to pray or meditate on it. Give thanks for the answer that will be revealed.

If you use an alarm, set it a little earlier than usual. You will want to have adequate time to record your dream after you awaken. Recording it is very important, as dreams are quickly forgotten. One method I use is to repeat the dream to myself silently before I get up, which helps to set it into memory. Then I write it down along with my associations and ideas about its meaning. Later, when I have more time, I return to the written account and work with it again.

Record your dream and work with it even if it does not seem to obviously answer your question. The answer may be couched in layers of symbolism.

Sometimes the dream oracle responds a night or two later with the answer. And sometimes the answer doesn't come in dreams, but in waking inspiration and intuition during the day. Your dreaming mind has worked on the question while you sleep; the answer is presented when it will have the greatest impact upon you. Answers may even come in synchronicities. When I do dream incubation, I never know how the answer will come—which is what makes this intuitive process so interesting. Sometimes I have a dream that addresses the question. Other times I remember little or no dream details, but have the answer clear in my mind as soon as I awaken. And still other times the answer is presented in an event days later.

Don't give up if you feel you're not making progress with the dream oracle. You may need to practice a little more. Try rewording the question. Reexamine your dreams to make certain you didn't overlook the answer. If an answer is not the one you're hoping for, it can be passed over.

As you become more adept at dream incubation, experiment with asking increasingly complex questions, such as "If Plan A doesn't work, should I try Plan B?" or "What should I do to accomplish my goal of _____?"

EXERCISE #2: SENDING MESSAGES IN DREAMS

Dreams are a natural medium for telepathy, the transferrence of thoughts between or among persons. Scientific experiments and research of dream telepathy have been done over the past century or so. The most famous—perhaps because the results were so well published—were at the Maimonides Medical Center Dream Laboratory in Brooklyn, New York, during the 1960s, under the aegis of Montague Ullman and Stanley Krippner.

In the experiments, a sender who was awake attempted to telepathically transmit an image, selected at random, to a sleeping recipient in another room. The subject was awakened and asked to describe any dreams. The next day, the subject would view several possible target images and rank them according to how well the images matched the content and emotional tone of their dreams. Overall, the results of these studies were significantly above chance. Researchers noted that teams who had a good rapport achieved better results.

For dream telepathy you will, of course, need a partner of any geographic distance. Decide who will be the sender and who will be the recipient. Set a date for dream telepathy: "Next Tuesday night I will transmit something to you." The sender should determine a time to transmit. Know the sleep habits of the recipient—there's no point in trying to send a message to dreams at midnight if the recipient is a night owl who stays up until 2 A.M. (The recipient may indeed receive the message, but the point here is to use dreams as the medium.) The sender may decide to set the alarm clock for a middle-of-the-night transmission.

Do not give the recipient any clues as to what will be sent. Have several possibilities available, and at the time of transmission, select one at random. Try the following, one at a time:

- A picture of a person or persons

- A picture of an animal

- A picture of a flower or object

- A word

- A short and simple message

- A longer, more complex message

Put several of each on pieces of paper. For images, you can clip ads and photos from magazines. Keep the papers facedown. Use one category at a time.

To transmit, center yourself with intuitive breathing and focus your intent upon connecting to the recipient. Hold a vivid mental image of the recipient in your mind; repeat his or her name silently three times. Shuffle your papers and select one. Focus upon it with as much intensity as possible for fifteen minutes. Make the image or words as vivid as possible.

The recipient carefully records dream recall upon normal awakening, and later reports the results to the sender. How well did you do? Keep a record.

Go through the complete list in the same roles. Then switch. Try other partners. Compare your results to your relationships. Do you have a higher rate of success with people who share a stronger emotional connection to you?

A variation of this is fun to try whenever you have the opportunity to travel to a time zone significantly different than that of your dream telepathy partner. Set an appointed time for transmission. The sender will focus on an image at random: "At 7 P.M. my time, which will be 1 A.M. your time, I'll send an image from whatever I will be doing at that moment." The receiver records any dream recall upon normal awakening. Later you compare results.

Try the above exercises with groups: one sender, several receivers. When the sender focuses on the image or message to be transmitted, he or she can connect with a group mind or consciousness. There is no need to link to each individual separately.

You can also experiment with unannounced dream telepathy. Make arrangements with a partner that at some unspecified time, you will send them an image or message. Contact them the day after and inquire about their dreams. How well do you get through when you are not expected? Permission in advance to try this is important, out of respect for the privacy of others.

Dream telepathy, like all intuition and psi development exercises, should be treated with consideration. Do not use it to send people angry or negative messages. Do not try to program or manipulate others with commands or suggestions. You will not be able to control people or make them do anything they would not ordinarily do.

Dream telepathy is an exciting tool for expansion of consciousness. Stay centered on personal growth, creativity, and helping others and your dreaming mind will respond with enthusiasm.

EXERCISE #3: DREAMING TRUE

You can also ask your dreams to show you the future. According to parapsychological research, extrasensory perception occurs to us more frequently in dreams than through any other medium.[1] An estimated 60 percent of precognition experiences occur in dreams.

Set your intention by asking your dreams to tell you something that will be helpful concerning the future, and that the dreams be literally clear and not couched in symbols. It is important to ask for helpful information; the dream oracle should be used for the highest purpose and not for entertainment. "Dreaming true," or dreaming the future, is distinctly different than ordinary dreaming. Such dreams often have their own peculiar trademark in emotional tone, atmosphere, signature imagery, or else a strong certainty upon awakening that the dream will come to pass. I stress *a* future, for the future is the outcome of probabilities, all of which are in constant motion.

I also caution that you not jump to conclusions when trying to dream true. A dream of an earthquake, for example, does not necessarily mean that a real earthquake will happen. An inner earthquake might be pending. Collective fears can influence our dreams, too. In the final years of the twentieth century, the media reported on a seeming increase in doomsday dreaming—dreams of natural disasters, wars, and so on. These dreams actually influenced some people to leave their jobs and homes in search of "safe" places. My feeling is that many of these doomsday dreams were reflections of collective fears about "the end times" because of this great turning of the calendar. You must be careful and responsible in interpreting your dreams.

I do believe that more and more, we will see futures in our dreams. We will pierce the veil of time as our intuition skills increase, as our consciousness evolves, and as our spiritual awareness increases. Our ability to look into probable futures will help us to make better decisions in the present. We cannot let our selves be governed by fear; rather, we must allow ourselves to be steered by Truth.

THE MORE YOU WORK WITH YOUR DREAMS, THE MORE YOU will appreciate them. Dreams really are your friends. They reflect what's going on within you. They serve the Higher Self, which constantly seeks the best for you.

Yes-or-No

SOMETIMES OUR INTUITION SPEAKS TO US DRAMATICALLY, other times subtly. In developing our intuitive ability, we hone our sensitivity to encourage the subtle signals to speak to us more emphatically. We learn our own intuitive language, and we train our intuition to add to its vocabulary.

One of the best ways to accomplish this is the yes-or-no format. Here are easy exercises that you can do on your own.

EXERCISE #1: STRENGTHENING YOUR INTUITION VOCABULARY

You must be thoroughly familiar with how your intuition speaks naturally to you when something is right or wrong. This is your own intuition vocabulary. Think of a decision you made, or a course of action that presented itself, that you knew—absolutely knew in every cell of your being—was right for you. What told you it was right? A strong physical sensation? A certain feeling? Visual or auditory clues experienced within, by the inner eye or inner ear? Approval from a guide figure or guardian angel you feel is around you? Reexperience the signals that say "right." Make a list.

Now think of a decision or course of action that was wrong. What signals did your intuition give you in that case? Reexperience, as vividly as possible, how your intuition says "wrong." Make another list.

In both cases, right and wrong, did you follow your signals or override them? What were the consequences of your actions? Think of other cases in which your intuition gave yes-or-no guidance. Did you receive the same kinds of signals?

Are you more likely to pay attention when your intuition says yes and disregard it when it says no? If so, you have plenty of company. It's not unusual to get guidance *not* to do something, but we proceed to do it anyway, because of all the "ought's" and "should's" our rational thought has lined up.

Resolve to follow your guidance, even when it runs contrary to the "ought's" and "should's." Make a pledge to yourself and your Higher Self in the form of an affirmation:

"I pay attention to my guidance and act in accordance with it."

Repeat this affirmation often on a daily basis.

Review your lists of signals for yes and no. Which are the strongest for each? Focus on those. Identify them with yes or no courses of action. Make more affirmations:

"When I experience _____ I know the answer is yes."
"When I experience _____ I know the answer is no."

For example, you might fill in the blanks with, "When I experience a sensation of expansion and light in my solar plexus, I know the answer is yes," and "When I experience a tightening in my solar plexus, I know the answer is no." You may have more than one signal for yes and no. It's best to work with one or two primary signals at first. You can always expand your vocabulary, as we will see in the next exercise.

Now put your intuition vocabulary into practical application. Every day, make decisions based upon your yes or no signals. Start with small decisions in order to build confidence: travel routes, clothing choices, purchases, food choices, tasks, and so on. Are the skies gray but the weather forecast calls for no rain? Your left brain says that you'd rather not carry around an umbrella if it's not necessary. But what does your intuition tell you? Keep a record of your activities. If you have any misses, analyze how and why you missed the signal. Did you allow any "ought" or "should" to creep in? Did you allow anyone to dissuade you from a course of action?

Gradually add more important decisions. The more you practice your yes-or-no guidance, the more natural the guidance will become, until you seldom have to stop and think about it. You will be naturally and confidently steered in the right direction.

EXERCISE #2: INCREASING YOUR INTUITION VOCABULARY

Practicing intuition exercises has shown you which sense is the dominant medium for you. Everyone is different. You have learned that your intuition speaks through images in the inner eye, sounds in the inner ear, feelings and emotions, or physical and tactile sensations.

In this exercise, you will expand your intuitive repertoire. Begin with your dominant medium. Choose a pair of opposites to represent yes and no. These will become new signals in your intuition vocabulary.

For example, if visual images are your dominant medium, you might work with:

—red and green traffic lights or flags

—the head and tail of a coin

—thumb up and thumb down

—up arrow and down arrow

—entry sign and exit sign

—smiling face and frowning face

—an open door and a closed door

You get the idea. If sounds are your dominant medium, pick sounds that are pleasing or harsh to you, or words that are opposite. For example:

—classical music and heavy metal music

—birds singing and jackhammers drilling

—a song you like and a song you don't like

—"yes" and "no"

—"right" and "wrong"

—"go for it" and "forget it"

Tactile and body sensations might be:

—feeling light and feeling heavy

—tingling and irritation

—expansion and contraction

—relaxation and tension

—energy and fatigue

—hot and cold

Feelings and emotions might be:

—happiness and anxiety

—eagerness and reticence

—joy and sadness

Be creative. Allow whatever arises *intuitively* to you to be your new yes-or-no signals. Put some fun into it. The Higher Self has a wonderful sense of humor and often speaks to us in puns and plays on words. Making it a game invites the Inner Child to play and opens us to territory where the intuition has freer reign to speak.

How would you use these opposites? When seeking intuitive guidance about a choice to make, ask, "Should I do such-and-such? Is this a go-for-it or a forget-it?" Or, "Is it heads up or tails up?" You'll have your answer.

EXPAND YOUR VOCABULARY EVEN MORE BY WORKING WITH signals that are not your dominant medium. If images are your strong suit, try working with sounds. After experimentation, you may decide that you prefer to stick with your dominant medium. But the more you listen to your intuition in as many ways as possible, the better a receiver you will be of all the guidance that comes from the Higher Self.

Card Games

CARDS ARE AN ENTERTAINING WAY TO TRAIN YOUR INTUI-
tion to see the invisible, sharpen your psychic ability, and send
your consciousness into archetypal realms.

Cards have served as an important tool in divination throughout history. The most widely used divination methods involve
interpretation of random patterns, such as stones, bones or sticks
that are cast, or cards that are selected. The random patterns organize information on an intuitive/psychic level.

In the exercises here, we are going to use cards for intuitive
"guessing" games, and for archetypal adventures that invite the
participation of synchronicity. You can do most of the exercises
by yourself; some can be done either alone or with a partner.

Games with Playing Cards

Obtain a deck of regular playing cards and a notepad for tal-
lying your results. Prepare yourself by doing intuitive breath
work. Spend a few moments stilling your mind.

EXERCISE #1: NAME THAT COLOR

This introductory exercise will get you warmed up with card games.

Shuffle the cards and hold them or place them facedown. Focus your sensory and intuitive attention on the cards until you feel that you "know" them. Focus on the top card. What color is its suit: red or black? Name the color and turn the card over. Were you right? Keep a record of your hits and misses.

You have one-in-two odds of being right by chance. Total your score. Twenty-six is chance. Are you above or below?

Do this exercise two or three times. You will then be ready to move on to the next levels.

EXERCISE #2: NAME THAT SUIT

Shuffle the cards and hold them or place them facedown. Focus on the card on top of the deck. What suit is it? Take your time with the answer. When you feel you have it, name the suit, and then turn the card over. Go through the entire deck in this manner.

Record each card: the suit you named and the actual suit.

How well did you do? You have a one-in-four chance of guessing the suit correctly. Therefore, out of fifty-two cards, you would expect to get thirteen correct by chance. Total your score of correct answers. Don't be dismayed if you scored less than chance! You probably are trying too hard. Relax and be detached from the outcome. You're not competing for a prize.

Now tally your hits of red versus black. Perhaps you said "diamonds" and the card was a heart. You intuited the color correctly, but not the suit. How many of your misses fall into this category?

Repeat this exercise daily and see how your score changes over a period of two weeks. Make notes concerning how you intuit the suits. Do you see mental pictures or have specific body sensations? Does your speed improve? Do you notice better results if you place your palm on top of the card while trying to "see" it?

EXERCISE #3: NAME THAT CARD

Shuffle the deck of cards and hold them facedown in your hands. Focus your intuitive attention upon them.

Instead of intuiting suits, name the suit and number or court figure: "jack of spades," "seven of hearts," and so on. Take as much time as you need with each card. Remain detached from the outcome. Anxiety and "trying" to be right will inhibit, not help, your performance. Keep a record of your choices and the results.

You will probably find that your score of hits drops considerably when you have to provide more specific information. The more you practice, the more it will come back up. Our intuition often gives us generalities. To become an intuition wizard, you want to hone your skills to intuit as much specific detail as possible.

Do this exercise daily for two weeks and keep track of your results. How much do you improve?

You may notice a curious phenomenon in this and perhaps in Exercise #2: you are one or two cards off from being correct. This is called "displacement" in psychical research: we get the correct information, but out of order or out of time sequence. Set your intention to be exactly on the mark.

EXERCISE #4: CARDS AT RANDOM

Instead of going through the deck in a top-to-bottom sequence, draw out cards at random facedown. Identify them and turn them over. Try drawing cards singly, or drawing several cards at a time.

EXERCISE #5: CARDS BY TELEPATHY

Variations of the previous exercises can be done with a partner. The object is to transmit information about the cards by telepathy. Our intuitive faculty is constantly picking up cues from the thoughts and feelings of others. This exercise will help you develop that ability to a higher level of skill.

Decide who will be the sender and who will be the receiver. Sit so that the receiver cannot see the face of the cards. You may sit opposite each other or in different places in the same room. You also can try sitting in separate but adjacent rooms—you must be close enough to hear each other speak.

Both parties should shuffle the deck before each exercise. This forms an energy partnership. Center yourselves with intuitive breath work and relaxation.

The sender keeps the deck facedown. He picks up the top card from the deck, turns it over, and focuses on the image: the color, the suit, or the identity of each card. The recipient should allow the information to arise spontaneously in awareness. When the receiver feels she knows the answer, she writes it down.

The sender keeps the cards in careful order, so that the first card on top of the deck becomes the last card in the stack. The results are then tallied.

Try exercises one through four with a telepathy partner. Change roles. Do the exercises as frequently as possible. Keep track of your improvement. Do you experience displacement with a partner?

Games with ESP Cards

ESP (extrasensory perception) cards are a small deck of symbols that can be used in intuition exercises similar to the ones already described.

ESP cards once were a standard tool in laboratory psychical research for testing ESP or psi. The cards still are occasionally used in controlled psi experiments, but for the most part, they have been replaced by the computer. They remain great for personal and in-home use.

The cards were originally named Zener cards after one of their creators. They were first used in 1930 at Duke University in North Carolina (the home of the Institute for Parapsychology and Rhine Research Center). They were created by two Duke faculty members, J. B. Rhine and Karl Zener, as a simplification of psi tests using regular playing cards. Psychical researchers had been using playing cards in tests since the late nineteenth century. The cards were made available for general public use in 1936.

A deck includes twenty-five cards of five symbols each: a star, an equilateral cross, a square, a circle, and a set of three wavy horizontal lines, like rippling water. Geometric shapes have proven to be particularly effective in intuition development.

Using ESP cards, you can do all of the exercises described for playing cards. You have a one-in-five chance of being correct.

You can obtain an inexpensive ESP card kit from the Institute for Parapsychology in Durham, North Carolina. Contact information is given in Appendix C. Or, you can invent your own symbols cards. Be sure that the card stock is thick enough to prevent any of the images from showing through the backs, and also that all cards are uniform in size.

Games with Tarot Cards

With Tarot cards, our game changes to more of an inner adventure with archetypal images. The Tarot consists of seventy-eight cards and is like two decks in one. A Major Arcana ("Big Mystery") has twenty-two cards bearing images, titles and numbers from zero to twenty-one. A Minor Arcana ("Little Mystery") has fifty-six cards that are similar to modern playing cards: there are four suits, and each suit has four court cards instead of three.

The origin of the Tarot is not known. It may have evolved from Renaissance playing cards and teaching aids that used images; or, it may have evolved from images used in magical and mystical paths that were popular then. It came into popular use for games and divination in the eighteenth century. Curious-looking, the cards caught the attention of occultists, who immediately seized upon them as books of secret learning. Most of the theories were more fanciful than factual, such as the cards originating in ancient Egypt or being spread around Europe by Gypsies who had found them in India. Those notions have long since been dispelled. However, the evolution of the cards does show a sophisticated influence of alchemy, magic, and the esoteric arts. Today the Tarot is a popular divination and inner work tool.

The language of the Tarot is archetypes: primordial images of unknown origin that have been passed down from an ancestral past that includes not only early man but man's prehuman and animal ancestors. Archetypes are not part of conscious thought, but are predispositions toward certain behaviors—patterns of psychological performance linked to instinct—such as fear of the dark or the maternal instinct, which become filled out and modified through individual experience.

Archetypes are endless, and appear in myth, folk tale, and fairy tale. Birth, death, rebirth, power, magic, the sun, the moon, the wind, animals, and the elements are examples of archetypes, as well as are traits embodied in gods and goddesses, the hero, the sage, the judge, the child, the trickster, the Earth mother, and other figures such as we find in the Tarot.

Archetypes contain more than can be described by words, which makes them ideal for the intuition. They communicate with the conscious mind in a numinous, or mysterious and transcendent, kind of way. Archetypes speak to us through dreams and through active imagination. When we work with the Tarot, we employ active imagination to engage with images in the archetypal realm. Our intuition loves to roam here. And, this inner work also stimulates our dream life.

The real power of the Tarot is not so much in divination, but in the expansion of consciousness into the archetypal realm, which is brimming and alive with spiritual energy, insight and creativity.

Tarot decks proliferate today, designed around themes such as angels and alchemy. The cards are steeped in symbols of an archetypal and esoteric nature. The Major Arcana is a collection of named and numbered images that portray stages of spiritual enlightenment. The images and their order are fairly consistent from deck to deck, regardless of theme. The Minor Arcana have various names for the four suits, which represent the elements, such as wands (air), staffs (fire), pentacles (earth), and cups (water). Some decks offer pictorial images for all of the Minor Arcana cards; many use repetitions of the suit signs and thus resemble like modern playing cards.

Tarot cards are excellent tools for personal spiritual and intuition work. You do not have to be a Tarot expert to enjoy working with the cards. I have used Tarot cards for many years and find them constantly refreshing and revealing.

For our exercises, we will use the Major Arcana portion of a deck. Select any deck that appeals to you—dozens are available on the market. Many are packaged with companion books that explain the cards. In particular, I recommend *The Alchemical Tarot*, created by my artist collaborator Robert Michael Place. Bob's knowledge of alchemy and his use of image and symbol are very effective for the type of work we will be doing here. Together Bob and I created a deck and guidebook package. We also developed *The Angels Tarot* set, which uses different angels to represent the archetypal qualities of the cards.

Each of the twenty-two cards in the Major Arcana is an archetypal image that symbolizes a quality, a state of consciousness, a stage of life, a characteristic, or a virtue. Each image has a central figure. For example, The Hierophant is a wise old teacher who symbolizes our higher wisdom obtained through learning and study. The Empress, a pregnant queen, represents our ability to bring forth abundance and to nourish others and ourselves.

The twenty-two cards also form a spiritual journey: our ups and downs as we attempt to move from ignorance to wisdom. We begin our spiritual journey as The Fool (numbered zero), who is untempered by experience, and end as The World (numbered twenty-one), a state of cosmic consciousness. Along the way, we experience our own magical power to manifest things in the material plane; we learn secrets and mysteries; and we experience unbridled ambition, profound love, material comfort, deprivation, pain, descent into our lower nature, redemption, and rebirth.

These stages of life and states of consciousness provide rich material for the intuition. By working with archetypal images, we invite the Higher Self to offer commentary on what we are doing in life.

The following is a list of the Major Arcana cards and their best-known names:

0	The Fool	11	Strength
1	The Magician	12	The Hanged Man
2	The High Priestess	13	Death
3	The Empress	14	Temperance
4	The Emperor	15	The Devil
5	The Hierophant	16	The Tower
6	The Lovers	17	The Star
7	The Charioteer	18	The Moon
8	Justice	19	The Sun
9	The Hermit	20	Judgment
10	The Wheel of Fortune	21	The World

Examine the cards closely. You will see that each card is a storyteller, and the story invites you to go deeper into the images. Take some time to familiarize yourself with them.

EXERCISE #1: MIRROR, MIRROR

Take the Major Arcana and get comfortable for meditation. Use intuitive breathing and relaxation to center yourself and quiet the mind. Turn over the top card on your stack.

Contemplate the image. Notice every detail. What does the card have to say to you? What is its story?

Imagine a gateway before you and allow yourself to become one with the card. What does the image have to say about you and to you? For example, how do you embody Justice? Perhaps it is a weak area for you rather than a strength. Does Justice have a "pay attention" message for you?

Allow your intuition to speak to you through the card. Ask for whatever is needed for you at this time. Thoughts and images will arise. Absorb them, but do not try to control or direct them. Take notes in your journal.

The mysteries in each card are vast, and in any one session, you will see only a small part of the whole. Perhaps you will be shown something related to a lesson you must learn in this life. Or, you will be given the answers to questions you have long sought. Perhaps you will be escorted to the cosmic Hall of Wisdom.

No two meditative excursions through the Major Arcana are the same, even with the same card.

Work with the cards one by one in order. Contemplate and meditate on one each day. After you've gone through the deck, continue to work with the cards when you feel drawn to them. Pull a card at random or select one that calls to you.

EXERCISE #2: ARCHETYPE FOR A DAY

Center with intuitive breathing and relaxation. Shuffle the Major Arcana. Set your intention with this affirmation: "*I will select the archetype I need to work with today.*"

Draw a card at random. As you did in the previous Mirror, Mirror exercise, contemplate the card and take notes of what it has to tell you.

As you go throughout your day, pay attention to how you encounter this archetype through synchronicity. Let's say that you draw Justice again. Perhaps you will see pictures, video or film of court scenes or depictions of justice or injustice. Perhaps you will engage in an argument and seek a solution of fairness. Perhaps you are confronted with someone's revenge as a way of justice. Perhaps you will intuitively know how to end a dispute.

At the end of the day, record your experiences in your journal. How did you live the Archetype for a Day? What insights and lessons did you learn?

EXERCISE #3: DREAMING THE TAROT

This exercise invites the intuition to work with both Tarot and dream images.

Before bedtime, shuffle the Major Arcana and select a card at random. Contemplate the card and what it has to say to you.

Affirm three times, "*My intuition will use (name of card) to give me a message in my dreams tonight.*"

When you awaken, record your dream and interpret it through dreamwork. The image of the card may not be present in your dream. Focus on the message of the dream and how it relates to the card.

YOU ARE LIKELY TO INVENT YOUR OWN EXERCISES WITH PLAYing cards, ESP cards, and the Tarot. Keep a notebook.

The Open Book

THE OPEN BOOK IS A GOOD SKILL-SHARPENING EXERCISE THAT you can do on your own.

You will need the white pages of any telephone book. Sit comfortably with the phone book on your lap or in front of you. Do intuitive breathing to center your consciousness and stimulate the third eye.

Close your eyes and open the phone book to any page. Run your finger down the page and stop wherever you wish. Using your inner vision, try to "see" the name your finger is pointing to. The response that arises spontaneously *first* in your mind is the answer. Do not try to "think" about it or make a rational guess ("Let's see, I should be in the M's, so maybe it's Madison . . ."). You want your intuitive mind, not your logical, deductive reasoning mind, to do the "thinking."

Open your eyes and compare your intuitive answer to the name your finger has selected.

You may find that you were wildly off the mark. Or you may be surprised at just how accurate you were!

Do the Open Book exercise for fifteen to twenty minutes several times a week. It's important to do it for a stretch of time—not just a minute or two—in order to get an intuitive flow of energy going. Vary the exercise by picking out phone numbers or addresses (such as the name of a street) instead of people names. Be adventurous and try for all three at once.

You may find yourself "seeing" the name just above or below the name your finger selects. This displacement is not uncommon in psychic work. The Open Book exercise will help you hone your accuracy.

Keep a record of your hits and misses, and observations you have around them. For example, your misses may occur when you allow guesses and deductive reasoning to sneak into the process. The record will show you how quickly you progress, and will increase your awareness of how your intuition speaks to you. Make note of emotions and physical sensations. Did you feel an electrical tingle whenever you "knew" you were right? Or a tightening sensation when you were wrong?

Do not be alarmed if you experience a period of many misses. The intuitive faculty goes through cycles of peaks and valleys, just as do our emotions, mental clarity, and physical energy.

You can try other books besides the telephone book for this exercise. The dictionary is a good alternative. Large scriptural works, such as the Bible, Torah, or Koran, are good. Avoid books that you read often and are very familiar with. Your memory of what material lies where in the book will interfere with the intuitive faculty.

The Future Newspaper

NOW IT'S TIME TO EXERCISE YOUR ABILITY TO SEE INTO THE future. The Future Newspaper exercise is based on a test once used in psychical research with mediums.

In the so-called newspaper tests, done under controlled circumstances, a medium would give information from the next day's newspaper before the newspaper went to press. Information included names of people featured in stories, page numbers, and positions of stories, headlines, news events, and so on. The information supposedly came from the medium's spirit helper, called a "control." The purpose of the newspaper test was to provide evidence in support of survival after death by showing that the information given at the sittings was beyond the subconscious knowledge possessed by either the medium or observers. In other words, it had to come from the realm of discarnate spirits.

These tests were especially popular after World War I, when many grieving families sought to communicate with victims of the war through mediums. Psychical researchers in turn sought to test the ability of mediums to try to find proof of survival.

The idea for newspaper tests came from Gladys Osborne Leonard, a famous British medium who had excelled at "book tests," or giving accurate information from books in distant locations. Leonard worked with a control named "Feda." Leonard was very good at her book and newspaper tests. The newspaper tests were especially significant because they were conducted before press time, and thus psychical researchers felt they could rule out clairvoyance. Apparently they did not consider that clairvoyance operates outside of linear time, and we can use this ability to see into the past and the future.

We have a much different and better understanding of psi today. Spirit guides and survival after death may have been the focus in those earlier times, but today we would look upon such tests as evidence in support of precognition and clairvoyance, something we can accomplish by projecting our consciousness.

In the Future Newspaper exercise, we are going to use our intuitive ability to read the news events that are yet to happen. Good intuition often involves sensing future events so that decisions in the present can be made accordingly.

RELAX IN A COMFORTABLE, SEATED POSITION AND DO INTUI-tive breathing as preparation for the exercise. Close your eyes and visualize before you the newspaper of tomorrow. Make the visualization as vivid as possible. Hold the newspaper; feel the texture and weight of it in your hands. Smell the newsprint and ink. See tomorrow's date clearly printed on the banner. Now read the major headline on the front page. What will tomorrow's news be?

Take a deep breath and let the image dissolve. Open your eyes and record your experience in your intuition journal. Make note of any physical or emotional sensations that are part of the experience.

On the morrow, check the newspaper against what you saw with your inner eye. How accurate was your vision of the headline? Did you see some of the same words, perhaps key words? Did you see a similar, but not same, event? Perhaps you saw news of an accident, but the kind of accident was wrong.

Do this exercise every day. The best time is in the morning, before you have been exposed to any news that might subconsciously influence you (such as the latest developments in an ongoing news story). Do not try to anticipate news based on knowledge you already have. As we know from experience, any day can bring surprises in the news.

Make the Future Newspaper exercise more complex as you progress:

—Increase the number of headlines you see. Note their position on the page. Open the newspaper and read different pages. Note the headlines and the numbers of the pages they are on.

—Read the stories under the headlines to learn details.

—Advance in time. See the newspaper that will be published in a week's time. Pick a date several months away and read that newspaper with the inner eye. Does your accuracy change the further out you move in time? Perhaps you allowed doubt about your ability to see the far future to affect your accuracy.

READING THE FUTURE NEWSPAPER HAS BEEN DONE SUCCESS-fully by many people looking for advantages for financial investment. For example, they seek to see stock quote prices on a given day. (See Chapter 11, Prosperity.)

The Future Newspaper also can help you plan your travel and make other decisions affected by news events.

Hide-and-Seek

How often have you had a sudden and unexpected thought about someone, only to find out later that they were thinking of you at about the same time? This sort of experience happens frequently, and is a splendid example of your intuition at work. You and the other person spontaneously used your intuition to tune in to each other. Perhaps your thoughts were colored by emotions or gave you a sense of what the other person might be doing. Perhaps you let the thoughts pass pleasantly, or perhaps you felt inspired to action, such as calling the other person.

This intuitive contact with another person can be deliberate as well as spontaneous. As we saw in the previous exercise, we can, through remote viewing (see Key #8), tune in to distant places and people.

EXERCISE #1: BASIC HIDE-AND-SEEK

Hide-and-Seek is a fun exercise that blends a childhood game with remote viewing. You'll need a partner. You can play this with a friend, family member, or spouse.

Select a day as Target Day. You must spend this day apart. One of you will be the viewer and the other the target. If you know your partner well, select a day that will *not* be one of routine activities that you can anticipate in advance. Ideally, you should not know where the target will be and what he will be doing.

At three agreed-upon check-in times, the viewer will attempt to intuitively see where the target is and what the target is doing. The target must jot down a few notes about his or her location and activities at the appointed times. Have no other contact throughout the day.

At the end of the day, compare notes. How accurate was the viewer? Were specific surroundings intuited? Colors? Emotional tones? Perhaps impressions were general rather than specific. For example, you might have received an impression of traveling while your target was on a bus, but no details about the bus or where it was going.

Did the target experience any unusual thoughts or intuitions at the same time? Was there a reciprocal remote viewing?

Try the exercise again on another day and switch roles. Vary Hide-and-Seek with other partners, including people whom you do not know well.

Here's how Hide-and-Seek worked for Jo, who used her intuitive remote viewing to tune in to a woman she knew casually. She did not know exactly where she, the "beacon," was located. Note how Jo allows her rational thought to interfere with and assess her intuitive impression:

> On tuning in to her, I rapidly had a very strong impression
> of whiteness, which then settled to a white house quite dis-
> tinctive in shape with eight or nine windows. There were
> some windows in the roof and an attractively shaped section
> where the roof met the vertical wall of the house. It was
> curved in the Dutch style. In the center of the main curve
> was an ornately outlined oval medallion shape.

Logic then started to invade. I kept thinking that the reason I was seeing something with a Dutch influence was because the beacon [target] was Dutch herself. But my first
impression was correct. The house did have a strong Dutch
style to it. I remember having an odd feeling in the solar
plexus as the first impression came in.[1]

Jo's first impression, which came rapidly, was of a Dutch-
style house. This was accurate. Yet she allowed her knowledge of
the target, a Dutch woman, to interfere with the impression.

It cannot be overemphasized that the impressions that arise
spontaneously and quickly are accurate. It is when we try to interpret or analyze them that we begin to distort them, at the risk
of accuracy. Note that Jo received a visceral, physical confirmation
of her first impression with an "odd" feeling in the solar plexus.
Do not ignore your signals. You do not know what you are "supposed" to intuit.

EXERCISE #2: FUTURE HIDE-AND-SEEK

Now we're going to stretch your intuition to look into the
future. Select another Target Day with your partner, but do not
discuss appointed check-in times or any planned activities. At the
start of the day, spend some quiet time in meditation, and center
with intuitive breathing. Select a time later in the day and ask
your intuition where your partner will be and what he or she will
be doing. Write down your impressions.

Check with your partner at the end of the day to see how your
advance impressions matched the events that took place. Do this
exercise often and switch roles and work with different partners.

Try looking further into the future. Pick a day a week away
or a month away and a specific time. Record your impressions.
On the Target Day, remind your partner to pay attention to

places, activities, and times. Then compare notes at the end of the day.

When looking into someone else's activities, it's important to do so *only* with their knowledge and permission. Developing the intuition is for our personal growth and betterment—and is part of our spiritual development as well—and is not for personal spy games.

Hide-and-Seek can help to foster a strong intuitive bond between people. The ability to tune into another person's safety and whereabouts can bring peace of mind when other means of communication aren't possible.

HOW TO TUNE IN

The Hide-and-Seek exercise will reveal to you the ways to tune in that work best for you. Experiment with these techniques:

—Visualize as vividly as possible the other person's face. Keep your attention to the face. You may not know what he or she is wearing. Allow those details to be filled in by the intuition.

—Mentally repeat the person's name. See the name written on your inner screen.

—Hold an object belonging to the person while doing one or both of the above. Or, look at a photograph of the person. The addition of psychometry can be helpful. However, you may not always have a personal possession or photograph to work with, so it is advisable to learn to do this exercise without having to rely on them.

—Hold a mental picture of the two of you linking hands.

—Imagine a searchlight emanating from your third eye, which travels across time and space and illuminates what you wish to see and know.

Messages in Voices

A PERSON'S VOICE CONVEYS FAR MORE INFORMATION THAN the words it expresses. We use our voice in many ways as part of our body language. The tone of our voice can add emphasis to our words or it can belie them. We respond instinctively to the sound and quality of voices. We respect and are swayed by strong, confident voices; we disregard weak and timorous voices. Often we are affected less by the actual words spoken and more by the sound of the voice.

As a writer, I interview many people of all walks in life for many purposes: fact-gathering, expert opinions, confidential perspectives, personal information, and more. I often interview people about intensely personal and sensitive experiences. In almost all cases, I am a stranger to them, someone they do not know personally, yet I am asking them to trust me in giving me the information that I seek. On numerous occasions, people have commented voluntarily to me that there was "something" in my voice that made them feel completely comfortable and at home with me.

The voice is an important key to intuition. The undercurrents of sound contain important information transmitted as impressions. The intuitive person learns to listen holistically, that is, to all the dimensions of the spoken word: the words themselves, and the information carried by the vibration of sound. In the cases described above, the interviewees' intuition tuned in to my voice and gave them impressions, perhaps telling them of my sincerity, interest, professionalism, or whatever that instilled in them a feeling of comfort and trust.

EXERCISE #1: VOICE ATTUNEMENT

This exercise can be done in pairs or in small groups. If done in small groups, keep the number to six or less in order to keep the flow of energy at a good pace. Prepare by relaxing, centering, and then doing intuitive breathing. While the others listen, one person speaks in a normal conversational tone. The person should begin by stating his or her name, followed by anything that comes to mind. For example, "My name is Edmund Smith, and I live in Rochester, New York. I work as a computer programmer, and I like to ski and play golf, etc." Or, "My name is Alicia Benton. Last Saturday I went to the Museum of Fine Arts and saw an exhibit of impressionist paintings. After that I had coffee . . . , etc."

It's important to state one's name, for we subtly convey much about ourselves in the ways we say our names. The rest of the little monologue provides time for the listeners to tune in to the voice. The speaker should talk for about a minute or so. Listeners may want to close their eyes in order to focus attention.

When the person is done speaking, the listeners then take turns giving their intuitive—and tactful—impressions that arose during the exercise. They may be impressions directly about the person, or they may seem to have little, if anything, to do with him or her. These should be offered, anyway, as they are likely to have a personal meaning to the speaker, perhaps relating to something they're thinking about, or a situation they're dealing with. For example: "While you were talking, I kept seeing an ocean liner . . ." You may find out the speaker has business dealings with cruise ships or is preparing to take a cruise vacation.

After everyone has offered their impressions, the listener provides feedback on the "hits." The listener should refrain from offering feedback, even in the form of expressions or nods of the head, until all have spoken. Otherwise, reactions might influence other participants to modify their reports of the impressions they received. Listeners should avoid labeling any impressions as "wrong." Rather, choose language such as "I don't feel that fits," or "I can't relate much to that." Sometimes we don't see the connections right way.

Go around the circle until everyone has had an opportunity to be the speaker.

Experiment with closing your eyes and keeping them open during listening. Closing them may help you a great deal, especially in the beginning, but you should increase your practice with them open. The reason is simple and practical. In everyday life, we converse with people with our eyes open. Trying to talk to someone whose eyes are closed is disconcerting at the least—we think we're boring them. Furthermore, our intuition also benefits from the visual impressions we receive.

After you've practiced with listening to short speeches, try a variation. The speaker simply gives his or her full name. That's it. You may think that just a name isn't enough to generate much in the way of impressions, but don't let yourself be limited. You'll probably surprise yourself with the amount of impressions you receive.

The truth of the matter is, you've been receiving such intuitive voice impressions all along whenever you interact with others. Unless these impressions were strong, they went unnoticed. Now you've expanded your awareness to take notice of them.

EXERCISE #2: VOICES ON THE TELEPHONE

Now try your voice attunement on the telephone. Listen to people with your intuition as well as your ears. What impressions do you receive? Jot them down while you are talking. If you have the opportunity, validate your impressions by asking questions.

In addition, you can exercise your intuition with these telephone games:

- When the telephone rings, identify the caller before you answer

- Or, identify the caller *and* the purpose of the call before you answer

- When you make a call, determine how many rings will sound before the call is answered

- Determine whether the call will be answered by a person or a machine or voice mail

- If any of various persons could answer the telephone, identify who will answer in advance

Of what benefit are voice impressions? They are especially useful when we meet someone for the first time, or when we are called upon to make decisions based on what we are being told. Can we trust someone? Have they done their homework? Impressions also help us to find the right words to say to another, especially in sensitive situations.

Colored Dots

IN TIBETAN DREAM YOGA, VISUALIZATIONS INVOLVING COL-ored balls of light are used, along with mantra and body positions, to facilitate lucid dreaming as a path to enlightenment. The dream yoga opens the inner eye. The two exercises here are reminiscent of dream yoga in that they employ colored dots or balls of light to focus attention inward. The inward focus encourages the intuitive faculty to expand.

EXERCISE #1: ORANGE DOT

For the Orange Dot exercise, you will need a piece of orange construction paper and one or more twenty-five–watt blue light-bulbs. The blue lightbulbs are not expensive, and you can find them in most grocery or variety stores.

Take the orange construction paper and cut out a circle about three to four inches in diameter. The easiest way to do this is to trace around the bottom of a drinking glass.

Select a room in your home where you will do this exercise. You will need to sit comfortably (not lie down) and look up at a wall. The objects and furnishings in the room will not matter, for your attention will be directed to the orange dot.

Tape the orange dot high up on a wall, but not so high that you have to crane your neck to see it from a chair or sofa. Arrange seating so that you face the dot.

Place one or two blue lightbulbs in the lamps in the room. The number of bulbs you need will depend on the size of the room. You will use only blue light to illuminate the room. The blue light will make it difficult to see objects in the room clearly, and the eyes will get tired quickly. Thus, external distractions will recede from attention and the inner eye will take over. The room will be dimly lit, but you should have enough blue light to see the orange dot on the wall.

With the blue light suffusing the room, settle comfortably into your chair or sofa. Relax and do some intuitive breathing to circulate the universal life force and open the third eye.

Focus your attention on the orange dot. Try to bring the orange dot off the wall and make it travel to your third eye. Spend twenty to thirty minutes on this exercise. If you lose concentration or can make the orange dot travel only partway, start again.

It is helpful to play some soft mediation music in the background. I use this exercise with a tape that plays about twenty minutes on a side. I do the exercise until one side is finished. The music helps me maintain concentration, and also not think about how much time is passing.

Initially, nothing may happen with the orange dot. Do not be concerned—just keep practicing. You will find that the orange dot will seem to expand or change shape, and will seem to come off the wall and travel in space. If you cannot bring it to your third eye, it does not mean you have failed the exercise. The act of focusing on the orange dot and attempting to bring it to your third eye is the essence of it. The inner eye will open. You may find intuitive flashes occurring to you while you do this exercise.

Do the Orange Dot exercise three or four times a week. I find that evening near bedtime is ideal. The exercise itself is very relaxing, and it also facilitates productive dreaming. Avoid the television, radio, or busywork after you're done.

If you don't have a blue lightbulb handy, you can still do this exercise effectively in regular but dim light. Blue light works a little more quickly.

EXERCISE #2: RED DOT

The Red Dot exercise is simple yet very effective. It requires nothing more than your imagination and can be done anywhere, anytime.

Relax with intuitive breathing. Close your eyes and imagine that a clean white screen covers your entire field of inner vision.

Now place a red dot or ball of light at the far left side of the screen. Slowly move the red dot in an arc across the screen to the right side. Then move the dot in an arc back to the left side, and so on, back and forth. Continue for as long as you can maintain concentration. If thoughts intrude, let them dissolve. Start over by establishing the clear white screen and red dot at the far left.

As in the Orange Dot exercise, moving the red dot will strengthen the inner vision. This is a great "inner eye calisthenic" that you can do in moments of idle time. Try starting the day with it.

Shapes and Symbols

THE VISUALIZATION OF GEOMETRIC SHAPES STRENGTHENS the intuition by exercising the right brain and training the mind to concentrate. A trained mind organizes information more efficiently, and organized information is simplified information.

Do these exercises during meditation. Like other exercises in this book, you can also do them during "downtime" such as waiting in a line or riding as a passenger in a vehicle.

CENTER YOURSELF WITH INTUITIVE BREATHING AND RELAXAtion. Close your eyes.

Imagine a black screen before you at eye level—like a blackboard at school. You are going to visualize a series of geometric shapes in white upon the screen. Hold each image steady for about three minutes, then move on to the next one.

Start with a circle. Place it in the center of your black screen. Hold the image still. If distracting thoughts arise, gently release them. You may find that the image wants to change by altering its shape or color, or moving around on the black screen. Whenever it shifts, gently return it to its original form. After you have held the white circle for several minutes, allow it to dissolve on the screen. Bring up another shape in white. Follow the same procedure.

Here are more shapes to work with:

- Circle with a dot in the center

- Square

- Square with a dot in the center

- Equilateral triangle

- Equilateral triangle with a dot in the center

- Equilateral triangle with a circle inside it

- Circle with an equilateral triangle inside it

- Circle with a square inside it

- Equilateral cross

- Square with equilateral cross inside it

- Five-pointed star

- Six-pointed star

- Cube

You can add your own shapes, perhaps symbols that are meaningful to you. For example, I often use a rose, which is the symbol of perfection. Stick to simple symbols that can be easily sketched in white upon your black screen.

Do as many shapes and symbols as you can in a session without becoming mentally fatigued.

Mirror Images

USING THE INTUITION MEANS BEING ABLE TO SEE, OR PER-ceive, the unseen. We "know" and we "see" what is not obvious to the physical senses and ordinary thought processes. In order for the inner eye to see better, we retrain the physical eyes to look beyond the physical.

One of the best and most often-used tools for inner eye train-ing since ancient times is the mirror, or any shiny, flat, and re-flective surface.

Gazing upon shiny surfaces is one of the oldest forms of *scrying,* a method of divination dating to the early Egyptians and Arabs. Throughout history, scrying has been used to look into the future, answer questions, solve problems, find lost objects and people, and identify or find criminals.

"Scrying" comes from the English word *descry,* which means "to succeed in discerning" or "to make out dimly." The tool of scryers, called a speculum, can be any object that works for an individual, but usually is one with a reflective surface. The oldest and most common speculum is still water in a lake, pond, or dark bowl. Ink, blood, and other dark liquids have been used by Egyptian scryers for centuries. Nostradamus scryed with a bowl of water set upon a brass tripod. The inside of the bowl was painted black. He would dip a wand into the water and anoint himself with a few drops, then gaze into the bowl until he saw visions.

Other specula include glass fishing floats, polished metals and stones, crystal balls, and precious gems. John Dee, the royal magician to Queen Elizabeth I, used a crystal egg and a black obsidian mirror. In Arab countries, scryers use their own polished thumbnails.

Inner eye exercises with mirrors are easy and can be done on your own. Do the following exercises in dim light. Remember from the Colored Dots exercises that dim light tires the physical eyes and thus enables the inner eye to take over. If you turn lights completely off and sit in the dark, you are more likely to get sleepy and doze off. Dim light will keep you mentally alert.

Do not try to anticipate or force results. Do not worry if nothing seems to happen. Like my experience in the psychomanteum, you may get your intuitive flashes afterward.

EXERCISE #1: FACES IN THE MIRROR

In a dimly lit room—a bathroom is ideal—sit in front of a mirror. Center and relax with intuitive breathing. As your eyes adjust to the light, regard yourself in the mirror. Focus on your face. Observe as much detail as possible—the contour and shape of your features, the angles of the face, the way your hair falls on the skin, and so on. Be detached, not judgmental. This is not an assessment of what you do or don't like, but a neutral observation of what is. In the dim light, your features will not be sharp and clear. Just observe.

Then pull back your perspective from detail to the whole. Look at your whole face. Hold the gaze as long as possible. When the image begins to blur, allow it to do so. If your thoughts wander, refocus on your face. Become aware of your breath. Continue the focus.

At some point, your awareness will shift. It may be sudden and marked, or it may be subtle and steal upon you. Your face may begin to change in the mirror, altering in shape or features. In fact, you may look completely different. Some people feel that the mirror reveals the faces of the people you were in past lives.

You may see other visions in the mirror—scenes, people, objects. You are likely to see these better with your averted or peripheral vision. Information, or an awareness, may come along with these visions. Take mental notes.

Or, you may see nothing in the mirror (except you), but instead have a flood of intuitive thoughts, inspirations, ideas, or knowledge. You may hear things distinctly with the inner voice, which may sound audible.

You will intuitively know when you are ready to stop the exercise. You will feel "full" or you will be tired. Recenter yourself with intuitive breathing. Then record your experience in your intuition journal.

EXERCISE #2: THIRD EYE GAZING

Sit comfortably in front of a small mirror. You can position a little mirror on a tabletop or dresser, or hang a small mirror on a wall at eye level. Dim the lights in the room. Relax and center with intuitive breathing.

Look into the mirror and focus your attention on the third eye, the spot in the forehead that is in the center of, and slightly above, the brows. Imagine a diamond of light there. Become aware of the breath, and feel the breath pulsing as energy through the third eye. Let thoughts dissolve.

Maintain the focus for as long as you can. The diamond of light may change shape or grow in size. Be aware of other imagery that may appear around you, or intuitive thoughts or words.

When you are ready to stop, recenter yourself with intuitive breathing. Record your experience.

EXERCISE #3: SCRYING FOR ANSWERS

Now that you've practiced seeing with the inner eye in mirrors, try your expanding intuitive ability on specifics, such as making decisions and seeing into the future. Formulate a single question to ask. (It's best to stick to a single question, especially in the beginning, in order to get the best intuitive response.) Examples are "Will I . . ." "Should I . . ." "Will Plan A be a success?" and so on. You can also ask questions about timing: "When should I . . ." Be very clear with yourself. If you're uncertain what to ask, your intuition will be uncertain how to answer.

Choose either Exercise #1 or Exercise #2. After you have settled in front of the mirror and relaxed, ask the question. Then focus your attention on the mirror. Keep the question foremost in your mind. Repeat it several times silently.

What response do you get? Images, thoughts, sounds, feelings? When you have the answer, you will know with a distinct signal in the manner that your intuition speaks to you, such as an aha! feeling, a tingling of the skin, or a warm feeling in the abdomen.

If you receive no answer while gazing into the mirror, remain confident that it will come at the appropriate moment.

Record your experience.

FOR A VARIATION OF THIS EXERCISE, MAKE OR GET YOUR OWN scrying tool. This can be any object with a shiny, reflective surface. Polished stones, crystal balls such as can be found in esoteric shops, polished silver bowls, or trays can all serve nicely. John Dee, the astrologer and magician who served Elizabeth I in the sixteenth century, used a mirror of polished obsidian for his scrying. This mirror is on exhibit today at the British Museum.

You can copy Nostradamus. Paint the inside of a small bowl black and fill it with water. Gaze into it. A mirror with its back side painted black will do the same job and is more convenient to carry and store.

If you use a scrying tool, you may find you get the best results if you look at the shiny surface at an angle so that you cannot see your own reflection. This leaves an open space for visions to form. The psychomanteum uses the same principle.

EXERCISE #4: MIRROR OF THE FUTURE

You can ask the mirror to show you the future—either yours or a more general future.

Follow the steps for Exercise #1 or Exercise #2. As you gaze into the mirror, state aloud your request. If you wish to see your future, say, "Reveal my future." If you wish to see any future events, perhaps unrelated to you, say, "Reveal the future." The request can be as specific or as general as you wish. Perhaps you might want to ask about the future of your country.

The mirror may respond with visual images, or you may receive a "knowing" within. Record your experience. Note any dates or time periods that you can check against the accuracy of what you are given.

NOTE: THE IDEA OF SEEING VISIONS IN A MIRROR MIGHT BE unsettling to some people in the beginning. There are many superstitions involving mirrors. If at any time you feel uncomfortable in a mirror-gazing experience—or any intuition exercise— simply stop. Remember that the intuition is part of you and is your friendly guidance, so there is nothing to fear from it. Movies and novels often portray the psychic realm as scary. It's simply territory that most of us aren't aware of. Once you explore the landscape, you will feel comfortable in it.

Lotus Eye

THE SIXTH CHAKRA, WHICH RESTS BETWEEN AND SLIGHTLY above the brows, is instrumental in our intuition and in the unfoldment of our spiritual vision. One cannot come without the other. The more we devote ourselves to developing the intuition, the more we increase our understanding of the spiritual or mystical side of life. If we devote ourselves first to a path of spiritual devotion and study, we find ourselves becoming highly intuitive and clairvoyant in the process. In either approach, it is the sixth chakra that becomes stimulated, and expands our vision of what we know about ourselves and our connection to the Source.

The sixth chakra is called the third eye because it sees the unseen. It is a lamp that illuminates the darkness of uncertainty around us. It is also called the lotus eye. In Eastern philosophy, the lotus represents beauty, sacredness, and the true nature of being. The chakras themselves are often portrayed as many-petalled lotus flowers. Think of the sixth chakra as a lotus flower opening to full bloom as you progress in your intuition development.

You will need a partner for this exercise.

Sit facing each other, close together, in a room with dim or blue light. If you have candles, place a lit one between you. If you wish, play soft, meditative music in the background. Relax and center with intuitive breathing. One of you will be the sender and one the receiver. Both of you know at the outset of the exercise that you will attempt to establish a link through your lotus eyes, and the sender will give a message to the receiver.

Set a timer for ten minutes.

Both of you bring your attention to the third eye of your partner. See it as a brilliant white lotus blossom unfolding its petals.

The person who is the receiver remains focused and passive.

The sender bathes the receiver in an energy of unconditional love. Appreciate the soul beauty of that person, wishing for him or her the highest possible good, the achievement of dreams, the enjoyment of love, prosperity, health, and happiness.

Then simply acknowledge the connection between the two of you, staying focused on the lotus eye. Intuitive impressions about the person may arise. Allow them to unfold. Make mental notes.

Keeping your attention on the lotus eye, keeping love and acceptance in your consciousness, send the partner a mental message. Direct it to their lotus eye. Keep it short—a word, a phrase, a sound, a picture. Do not try to preconceive a message in the beginning. Allow whatever is appropriate to arise intuitively during the course of the exercise. Be absolutely sincere. Put as much energy as you can into it.

When the timer sounds, both recenter with intuitive breathing. Compare experiences. The receiver speaks first, describing feelings, thoughts, images, tactile sensations, and impression of a message. Don't guess or try to fill in where nothing was experienced. If there was no distinct impression of a message, say so.

The sender then describes his or her experience and intuitive impressions and states the message. The receiver may discover that the message was cloaked in symbols, feelings, or other intuitive imagery.

Now switch roles and do the exercise again, setting the timer for ten minutes.

Most people have at least some difficulty in understanding the message. Do this exercise frequently, with different partners, to increase your skill. What you are learning is telepathy, the sharing of thoughts, which is a function of the third eye. You are learning how to "read" people without speaking.

The purpose of this exercise is not to invade the thoughts of others, but to accurately sense what they are thinking or feeling, so that you can make the best possible response. People often say one thing when they really mean another. Or they don't say what they really want. The best negotiators and the best salespeople have keen intuitions in that they sense the full meaning behind the words of others. They see the big picture. Their keen lotus eye gives them clues as to what to say or do to encourage others to respond favorably. They know when to keep pressing and then know when to quit.

THE LOTUS EYE EXERCISE ALSO HELPS YOU TO CONVEY YOUR message—your conviction, your feelings, your persuasion, your ability, your sincerity—to others in powerful, unspoken ways. Intuitive ways. Sometimes people are not swayed so much by your words as by a "feeling" they have about you. It's called charisma. Like the blossom of the lotus, it's waiting to unfold in you.

॰ PART III

Using Your Intuition

Chapter Seven

Practical Intuition

CONGRATULATIONS ON DEVELOPING YOUR INTUITION! You've probably already discovered ways to put your intuition to use.

Intuition works for us all the time, arising spontaneously as we need it. Now that you've practiced the exercises in the 22 Keys, you've gotten better in touch with your intuition and how it speaks to you. You should be reaping the benefits of it daily.

Intuition is not just reactive, it is proactive. You can ask your intuition to help you on demand, anytime you need to make a quick decision about small matters, or whenever you face choices about something important. You can also ask your intuition to help you improve your relationships, improve your finances, expand your creativity, and further your self-improvement. Your intuition can assist you in healing. And, it can help you break through to a new level of visionary thinking.

There are four basic applications that your intuition serves in all areas of life:

- Make a decision
- Find a solution to a problem

- Receive general guidance for goal-setting and action

- Enhance creativity

AN INTUITION ACTIVATION PLAN

Regardless of whether you are dealing with a personal need or a situation in business, follow these steps to activate your intuition:

1. Set a clear objective. We're not always clear with ourselves as to what we're looking for or what we need. Situations can be a tangle of short-term and long-term needs or even conflicting needs. You must be clear about your central purpose. "My objective is to be the top-ranking salesperson in the company." "My objective is to improve my marriage." "My objective is to inspire people with my work."

2. Ask a clear question. As a beginner, you are likely to get the best results with questions that can be answered with a yes or no. "Should I take over the XYZ account?" "Should I take the job offer?" "Should I ask my spouse to see a counselor with me?" However, as you gain more intuitive experience you can pose questions that are more complex: for example, "Tell me the best way to . . ." or "How can I . . ." For example, "Tell me the best way to achieve my sales objectives."

3. Gather data. Intuition does not operate in a vacuum. It helps you make better sense or see more clearly—or go beyond—that which you already know and understand. Information is your best friend. Do your research and your homework thoroughly.

4. Ask for guidance. Seek out the opinions of others. Ask for inner guidance.

5. *Evaluate what you have gathered.* Your rational mind will leap to the chance to sift and sort. But allow the intuition to play a strong hand. Sometimes the facts and figures look good, but don't "feel" right.

A successful senior vice president of finance I know uses his intuition all the time in evaluating numerous financial decisions for his company. Big money rides on these decisions, which involve not only questions of yes or no, but also timing. John examines data and pays attention to his gut response. "Sometimes something just doesn't feel right, no matter how good it looks," he said. "When that happens, I pay attention and investigate. The first thoughts that rise in your head are the best. I rely a lot on that when I do an analysis."

6. *Take action.* Follow through. You'll benefit from the process only if you act on it.

In this section, you'll find a collection of exercises and guided meditations to help you in all areas of life. Use them, and let them inspire you to develop more exercises of your own.

Chapter Eight

Getting the Message

HERE ARE SOME EXERCISES THAT WILL STIMULATE INTUITION breakthroughs to give you a helping hand. Use them for any situation. Set your objective and question. Prepare for each exercise with the intuitive breathing and relaxation for meditation techniques found in Keys #1 and #2.

EXERCISE #1: CALLING THE INNER GUIDE

Close your eyes and let yourself travel to a beautiful garden. The sun is shining, the air is warm, and all around you flowers are in full bloom. Relax and appreciate the peace and beauty. Let all of your senses drink in your surroundings. You are on a little path that meanders through the garden. Walking along, you see a small bench ahead of you on the side of the path. Sit down on the bench.

You notice a presence approaching you along the path. It may be a person. It may be an animal. It may be someone or something mysterious—perhaps an angel or a spirit guide. This is the inner guide you have chosen to represent the wisdom of your Higher Self.

Greet your guide with a welcome and thanks. Ask for its name.

Your guide has a message for you. It is precisely what you need to know, the answer to your question. Receive the answer and thank your guide for helping you.

Return now along the garden path. Recenter yourself, and when you're ready open your eyes. Write down any additional thoughts.

Once you have made contact with the Inner Guide, you can summon its help anytime by calling to mind an image of it, and/ or calling its name. ("Help me out here, Inner Guide . . .") Names are particularly important. In mystical and magical traditions, names provide access to power.

You can have many Inner Guides. You may work with a group of them, or one that periodically gives way to another. For example, sometimes when I summon the Inner Guide a leopard answers the call. Other times it is an angel that responds. I have also been aided by an owl and a wise old man who wears a triangle-shaped crown upon his head.

In addition to receiving a message from your Inner Guide, you can carry on a discussion with it.

Once you have made contact with your Inner Guide, do not be surprised at encounters in other ways, such as in dreams and synchronicities.

EXERCISE #2: E-MAIL FROM YOUR HIGHER SELF

Close your eyes and imagine yourself at your desk at home or at work. Sit down at your computer and go on-line to the Internet. You are informed that you have e-mail waiting. Open your mail. You have one letter—it's from your Higher Self.

The letter answers your question. It may be with a single

word. Or, your Higher Self may have written you a longer letter full of advice and insight.

Read the letter and save it in a special file. Send a reply note giving thanks.

Recenter yourself and when you feel ready open your eyes. Write down any additional thoughts.

As in the prior exercise, you can carry on an e-mail correspondence with your Higher Self.

EXERCISE #3: PHONE CALL FROM GOD

Close your eyes and imagine yourself comfortable at home. The telephone rings. You answer. God is calling you with the answer to your question.

When the message is delivered or the conversation is completed, give thanks and hang up. Recenter yourself and when you feel ready open your eyes. Write down any additional thoughts.

EXERCISE #4: MESSAGE IN A BOTTLE

Close your eyes and imagine your self at the seashore. You are alone, walking along the beach at water's edge. You feel relaxed and at peace, enjoying the crunch of the sand and the cool water lapping at your feet. The air is full of the smell of salt.

Looking down, you notice something shiny just ahead of you. You pick it up. It is a bottle, brought in by the tide. It is sealed and has something inside of it—it looks like a piece of paper.

You open the bottle and pull out the paper. It has a message written on it. The message is addressed to you and answers your question. You are elated. The universe has sent you a letter. Looking down again, you see a whole sand dollar. It is your lucky sign that this message is indeed right for you.

EXERCISE #5: OUT OF THE WOODS

Sometimes situations are so complicated or have so many ramifications that it's difficult to get a handle on them. We think that if only we could see things more clearly we would know what to do. This exercise will help you "see the forest for the trees" and find your way to a clearing.

Close your eyes and imagine yourself inside a dense forest. You are looking for a way out. It seems that you have been searching for a long time. All the trees look the same.

You find a fallen tree and sit down on it to rest and think of a new strategy. Suddenly your attention is drawn to a large tree in front of you. It is a beautiful tree, majestic, and very old. It is a Tree of Knowledge. You become aware that it wishes to communicate with you.

The tree tells you that there is a solution to your dilemma. There is a way out of the forest. You listen carefully as the tree tells you where to find a path. You thank the tree for its help, and, following the instructions, you find the path and are able to leave the forest.

At the edge of the forest is a beautiful clearing. You feel wonderful as you enter the clearing. All of the twists and turns and darkness of the forest have been left behind. You turn and look at the forest. Before, it was a maze of trees. Now you can see it and the trees within it with great clarity.

Standing in the clearing, you are warmed by the sun. Its light brings illumination to you. You realize that you now know what to do. What are the impressions that are presented to you?

Recenter yourself and open your eyes. Write down your impressions. Perhaps a solution has been made obvious to you. Or, use free association to obtain more information from your impressions.

Use your imagination—and your intuition—to create other exercises in which you "get the message."

Body Wisdom

The body is one of our best intuitive barometers of what is right or wrong for us. You already know from your own experience, and from your practice of the 22 Keys, that your intuition gives you many signals through your body.

Your body also is your last line of defense when you fail to recognize other intuitive signals that something may not be right for you. Health issues often arise because we need to pay attention to something else in life.

It has been well-documented that stress is a major factor in many health issues. When we are stressed, the body speaks back very plainly. And, if we do not honor our gifts and talents, thus creating an imbalance in our life, our bodies will speak up about that, too.

People who pay attention to their intuition learn to listen to their bodies as well. Everyone has his or her unique talents and purpose in the world. When we are in harmony with that, our bodies function well. When we fall out of harmony, our bodies tell us so. (I am not attempting to offer a simplistic explanation for illness, however. There are many reasons why people get sick. But when we are emotionally out of whack, our bodies respond accordingly.)

Think of all the ways that language uses the body to describe negative emotional—and intuitive—reactions:

- He is a pain in the neck

- This makes me sick to my stomach

- I'm breaking my back to get this done

- This assignment is a major headache

- I'm knocked flat

- I'm too paralyzed to do anything

You may have noticed that when something is not appropriate for you, you receive an intuitive signal via your body. Sometimes this signal is a significant distress. Christiane Northrup, author of *Women's Bodies, Women's Wisdom*, noted that one of her medical student friends who had a "bad back" always experienced a flare-up of pain when she had to do something she did not want to do:

> Currently, she is contemplating writing a research paper.
> Whenever she thinks about writing this piece and the col-
> leagues with whom she will be involved, she gets neck pain
> and feels sick to her stomach. All her training has taught her
> that publishing this research paper is what she should do for
> her career. Yet her inner guidance, which speaks to her
> through her body's feeling, is telling her something quite
> different. She knows that she must take the radical step of
> choosing between her inner guidance and what society is tell-
> ing her is best if she is to remain healthy.[1]

Note the conflict between the body's intuition and the rational mind's "should." We do this all the time to ourselves— telling ourselves why we "must" or "should" do something that we clearly do not wish to do, or is not in our best interests. Even when our body tells us differently, we often ignore it, treating the symptoms instead to try and make them go away.

Resolve to pay more attention to how your body speaks to you. Relate your body talk to your true feelings and emotions. Take appropriate action. It's not always possible to remove yourself entirely from a situation or relationship. However, there is always something you can do to bring yourself into better balance.

Chapter Nine

Problem Solving and Decision Making

PROBLEMS THAT DEFY SOLUTIONS ARE VEXING AND CAN even undermine our self-confidence. The number one rule for intuitive problem-solving is to relax and know that for every problem there is the perfect solution. It's simply a matter of seeing the answer.

Always approach problems from the highest perspective, not the lowest. If you are mired in mud, so to speak, you will not see the brilliance of the sky.

We are often called to make decisions in which the various options are neither obviously right nor wrong. Each option has its good points and its bad points. Which is the better—or best— way? Without the intuition, we can go round and round in circles. Try these exercises when you feel stuck.

First, write up short summaries of each of your options and list their advantages and disadvantages. Also list your thoughts and feelings about each one. Give a title to each option.

EXERCISE #1: BRAINSTORMING OUTSIDE THE BOX

When we get buried in difficulties, it's hard for the rational mind to sort through everything. We have to make decisions, but nothing seems clear. We become afraid of making the wrong decisions. Result: paralysis.

The intuition is a sharp blade that cuts through mental and emotional clutter.

The first step in problem-solving is to look for the most obvious and viable solutions, a process that engages the rational mind. Then we look beyond, especially if there are no good obvious solutions. This is called "brainstorming outside the box." We offer what comes up freely without judgment or concern as to whether it is feasible, practical, or even possible. Nothing is mocked or discredited. Sometimes the most unlikely suggestion leads to the hit that provides the solution. In a group think tank, participants speak out on whatever comes to mind. If you are brainstorming outside the box by yourself, jot ideas down in a list. Hold nothing back.

Compose a clear question about the problem that needs to be solved.

Finish one or more of these sentences in as many ways as possible:

In my wildest dreams I would like . . .
If anything were possible, then . . .
If money were no object, then . . .
In a perfect world . . .
I would live happily ever after if . . .

EXERCISE #2: FREE ASSOCIATION

Free association is a well-established exercise used in business, politics, therapy and counseling, dreamwork, creative expression, and self-improvement activities. It is an excellent tool for problem-solving and decision-making. Use free association in all of these practical application exercises in this book.

Free association is very simple. For example, let's say that your intuition gives you a symbol, a visual image, or a word or phrase. Write it down on a piece of paper. What else does it make you think of? Jot down your impressions quickly. Don't stop to think about them or analyze them. You will do that later. Your first impressions will give rise to secondary impressions. Record those as well. Soon you will have mapped out quite a few associations.

Continue with the free associations for as long as the energy carries you. Perhaps you will stop when you get a burst of insight that makes everything fall into place. Free associations often reveal to us our true thoughts and feelings. Analyze them and see what they have to tell you.

EXERCISE #3: FORK IN THE ROAD

Close your eyes and see yourself traveling down a straight road. Whether you are walking or riding, you are proceeding carefully.

You come to a place where the road forks. There are as many branches of the road as there are options before you. From left to right, name the forks in the road with the titles of your options.

One by one, look down each fork. Notice the appearance of the roads—are they well maintained, or are they filled with ruts and holes? What is the condition of the surrounding environment? Is the road in a desolate place or does it go through attractive scenery? Is the road straight, curved or hilly?

Now take notice of your thoughts and feelings about the forks. Does one attract you while another repels you? Does one look safe and another dangerous?

What other details do you notice about each fork in the road?

Reassess your options, using both your logical analysis and your intuitive impressions.

EXERCISE #4: AT THE CROSSROADS

This exercise is useful for situations in which we're trying to decide about major changes in direction in life. We might be considering changing jobs or careers, moving to a new city, getting married or divorced, and so on. We might be considering making a major commitment of our time, energy, and resources.

To begin, draw up lists of the pros and cons surrounding your decision. Now list your hopes and fears. Take a piece of paper and draw a crossroads intersection. The road you've been traveling is at the bottom. It represents what's behind you and also the path you are on. The road at the top represents the continuation of your present journey—if you made no changes, you would keep going in the same direction. To your right is the road that represents the change that you are considering. To your left is a mystery road—another direction unknown or not yet explored.

Close your eyes and imagine that you are traveling on a straight road. You arrive at a crossroads and stop. You have the option of continuing in the same direction, or taking an entirely new road. Which will it be?

As in the previous exercise, examine each road. How do their appearances and surrounding environments compare? What are your thoughts and feelings—can you see your hopes or fears down any road?

Look carefully at the road on the right. When you feel you have examined it thoroughly, look at the road on the left. This is the unknown. It may represent an alternative that you have not considered. It may also represent information that you have overlooked. What do you see? Accept whatever arises spontaneously to you.

Do not be alarmed if the road remains dark. It simply means that nothing new wishes to present itself.

MEDITATIONAL EXERCISES SUCH AS THESE OFTEN HAVE A WAY of taking on their own life. For example, you might find yourself approached by a personification of your Inner Guide, who gives you a message or instructions, or who engages you in conversation. You might find yourself approached by other people who are involved in the decision. Allow your inner vision to unfold. You are not obliged to stick to any script. Trust that you will receive what you need.

EXERCISE #5: A SPIRITUAL APPROACH

In his classic book *The Power of Positive Thinking*, minister and motivator Norman Vincent Peale told of the numerous politicians, leaders, and business persons he knew, many of them super achievers, who often turned to prayer in order to obtain guidance in problem-solving and decision-making. The great motivator Dale Carnegie would leave his office when times were busiest and most pressured and would visit a nearby church, where he sat quietly in prayerful meditation. Such a break stills the mind and enables needed insight to come through.

For Leslie, prayer opened the door to the guidance that set her back on the right track when she found herself at a low point in life:

A relationship that I had thought would be permanent was ending, I hated my job, I didn't like my living arrangements, and a general dissatisfaction with my life was causing great despair. One cold November Sunday night I went to church. The auditorium was very large, seating between one thousand and two thousand people. On this night, attendance was sparse, and I sat on next to the last row with no one nearby.

Waiting for the service to begin, I remember thinking to myself, "God, what am I going to do?" A clearly audible voice said, "Go back to school." The voice was so clear I turned around to see who sat behind me. To my surprise, there was no one there.

I had never considered returning to school as a possible response to my situation, but the advice made such good sense that I quit my job, stored my furniture, and within three months was back in college as a full-time student. The fact that I had only seven hundred dollars to my name never seemed like an impediment, and of course, it wasn't. I was able to get loans and find jobs and assistantships all the way through my master's degree. Sometimes the work came in ways that were truly miraculous. My guardian angel seemed to be working overtime.

The truly amazing aspect of this experience was that I did not think it unusual or strange in any way. I never told anyone of the experience until years later, after I had become involved in a spiritual search. Only then did I truly recognize how I had been blessed, and I was amazed that I had the good sense to follow the guidance. I am very happy that I listened and acted.[1]

Let's analyze the situation:

- Leslie felt she could not sort out a solution to a confluence of overwhelming problems.

- She went to church to ask God for guidance. Settling into prayer placed her mind in a quiet and receptive state, making her more open to her intuitive guidance.

- She asked a question, which organized her inner resources.

- She heard the answer as a voice. For Leslie, this was God's answer delivered by her guardian angel.

- The answer surprised her, as the intuition often does. It presented her with information she had not considered. Rather than dismiss the guidance, however, Leslie followed it.

Questions to Ask Yourself

Here are suggestions to help you frame questions for solving problems and making decisions:

- What is the best solution/decision for me/for everyone?

- How can I implement the solution?

- What are the obstacles to a solution?

- Should I follow Plan A?

- When is the best time to _____?

Finding Your Purpose and Achieving Goals

FINDING ONE'S PURPOSE IN LIFE RANKS AS THE NUMBER ONE reason why people seek intuitive consultations and psychic readings. Sooner or later, everyone wonders if he or she is pursuing the right career. Sooner or later, people feel stuck in their jobs or at a dead end and wonder what else they should do. Uncertainty about the direction of one's life always occurs during times of major change: loss of a job, death of a loved one, divorce, children leaving home, accidents and illness, and other upsets.

People often think that in order to find their true purpose they have to wipe the slate clean and make a radical change. Sometimes that's the case, but it's not always the best answer for everyone. Finding your true purpose can come through a hobby or volunteering or an activity or a change in the duties of your present job. A change in perspective can change your life as well. For example, I've met many people who suddenly feel called to become healers. They think that the way to accomplish this is to quit their job and open a retreat center in the mountains. Usually they haven't thought through how they are going to arrange financing, run a business, attract customers, and handle the day-to-day administrative matters.

There are many ways to become a healer. You can take classes to learn a variety of energy healing modalities that will enable you to do healing as a lay practitioner. You can volunteer for a hospital, nursing home, or hospice.

More important, however, is a shift in perspective to seeing that healing begins at home and in daily life. No matter what we do, we can aspire to bring healing energy to it. If you want to change "the system," don't abandon it. Work from within it to change it for the better.

BUILDING YOUR INNER ROAD MAPS

Realizing your highest potential and dreams is accomplished with the help of inner road maps built by intuitive guidance. Your intuition will help you see clearly where you are going and where you want to go (often the two are not the same). You will receive course corrections when the timing is right, thus avoiding delays and recovery time. And, your intuition will show you just how rich your path through life is: there are many possibilities and many choices.

Exercises

EXERCISE #1: GOING TO GROUND ZERO

Time is a great motivator to get our priorities in order. We know that our time on this planet is finite, but we live like we have endless time. We may in fact know what it is that we want to do, but we put it off while we do other things. Our life becomes full of "when's": "When such-and-such happens, then I will . . ."

We convince ourselves—and anyone who will listen—that when the timing and circumstances are perfect, we will make our move.

Perfect circumstances seldom, if ever, arrive. If you are waiting for perfect, it's not going to happen.

If you were told that you had only one more year to live, what would you do? Would you stay in your job, stay in your marriage, continue to live in the home you don't like? Or would you go to "ground zero" and do what would matter to you most?

For this exercise, assume that you have one year left and money is no object. Take a piece of paper and list all of the things that you would do. Then list all of the things that you would let go. In both lists, circle the things that elicit your strongest emotions.

Now take another sheet of paper and list all of the obstacles that stand in your way: fears, practical matters, beliefs, and so on. Take them one by one and write down why they are reasonable or why they are not.

Finally, list your solutions—what actions can you take to remove your obstacles? Ask your intuition for help. Do free associations with your impressions.

Develop and implement a plan of action.

EXERCISE #2: SETTING GOALS

In order to reach a goal, you have to know your starting place. This requires an honest self-assessment. Take a sheet of paper and write down your goal. Be very specific. Then make a statement about where you are now. Be candid about your thoughts and feelings. Are you really ready to reach for your goal? Are you prepared to make the necessary changes and even sacrifices? For example, you're not going to attract wealth if money runs from your fingers. You won't find your ideal partner if you don't have a lot to offer yourself. And you won't get your degree if you don't enroll in a program and study.

Close your eyes and ask your intuition for guidance on how to get from point A to point B; record your impressions and interpret them. You can also ask for a time line—such as how long it will take you to accomplish your goal.

Develop and implement a plan of action.

Don't overlook smaller daily goals—they are just as important as long-range goals.

EXERCISE #3: CREATE THE FUTURE YOU WANT

Superachievers don't wait for events—they make events happen. What do you want your future to bring? What would you like to be doing a year from now, five years from now, ten or more? Draw up a list of everything you would like to see come to pass in your relationships, career, home, health, and interests. Be bold! You have the power to set forces in motion that will help you achieve your dreams.

With the help of your intuition, set your goals and objectives. Visualize yourself as already accomplishing them now. Create affirmations to support your goals. Impress your thoughts every day with your visualizations and affirmations. Believe in them, and act as though you have reached your goal.

"The man who assumes success tends already to have success," said minister and motivator Norman Vincent Peale. "People who assume failure tend to have failure. When either failure or success is picturized it strongly tends to actualize in terms equivalent to the mental image pictured."[1]

For Peale, the formula was simple: Prayerize, Picturize, Actualize. He would pray to God for guidance about everything in life. When he felt clear on a goal, he built a mental picture of it already accomplished. He believed with all his might that it would come to pass and that God would help him accomplish the goal. Then he acted as though the outcome had already happened. And, he did whatever he could to help bring the goal into reality.

Actor Jim Carey, one of the highest-paid actors in Hollywood, was struggling in obscurity when he wrote himself a check for $10 million and proclaimed that it was his earnings. It was a powerful image, and Carey, believing in himself, worked hard to make it come true. In fact, when he became a star he earned far more than $10 million for a single movie.

Expect the best, and you will get the best.

If you are having difficulties with your self-confidence, then you must first use visualizations and affirmations to build yourself up. Bolstering your faith in yourself may take time and effort, but the payoff is well worth the investment. Here are some tips that will help you:

Everyone excels at something. What are your strengths and talents? Build powerful visualizations of your excellence. See yourself being recognized and appreciated by others. Change your behavior: act as though you are indeed worthy of respect and admiration.

Extend your excellence to new areas. Don't be afraid to try something new. Ralph Waldo Emerson advised, "Do the thing you fear, and the death of fear in certain." Even if you don't succeed at first, you will gain in self-confidence.

An author I know decided to step out on the lecture circuit. She set a high fee for herself despite the fact that as a speaker she was an unknown. But she had confidence in her ability to command an audience and thus command the fee—and she did.

Remember that whatever you are doing now, you are capable of much more.

EXERCISE #4: GIVE YOURSELF THE GREEN LIGHT

You can make productive use of that time spent waiting at red traffic lights. While the light is red, focus on a goal you wish to obtain. When the light turns green, congratulate yourself on obtaining the goal.

EXERCISE #5: GIVE YOURSELF A PSYCHIC READING

We tend to believe what we are told, especially by authority figures. Such words create images and attitudes that become impressed upon us, for better or for worse. For example, the placebo effect has been well documented in scientific studies: people who strongly believe they have been given a medication will react accordingly, even if they have been given only a sugar pill.

People sometimes seek out an intuitive consultant or psychic in the hopes of having their questions answered about what they should do and what will happen to them. A good reading can help the client obtain valuable insight.

Just as effective, however, is your own self-directed reading. You play the role of both client and psychic. The reading is an entertaining way of fueling your visualizations and affirmations for success. It taps into your intuitive wisdom.

You will want to tape record your reading so that you can listen to it again.

Write out a list of questions to ask in the reading. Then assume the role of the reader. You can get as much into the spirit of the play as you wish: assume a name, put on a special outfit, light candles and incense, and so on.

Prepare yourself with your intuitive breathing and meditation procedures. Then go down the list of questions and give the answers that you want to hear. Tell yourself how wonderful you are, and that you are going to achieve your objectives. Allow whatever arises spontaneously to be your guidance. Put as much positive energy as you can into your reading.

When you are done with your reading, meditate for a while, holding vivid mental images of your "predictions" coming true.

Listen to the tape repeatedly to keep the energy flowing.

EXERCISE #6: LETTERS FROM ABOVE

A variation of the self-directed psychic reading can be done in journaling, by writing letters to yourself from God, spiritual figures, saints, or angels. Address the letters to yourself personally, such as, "Dear Marie, This is your guardian angel speaking. . . ." Deliver answers to questions and guidance. Allow your writing to flow freely and spontaneously—remember that the first thoughts are the best. This is a form of automatic writing, which is a way to access your intuition, Higher Self, divine guidance, and deep creativity.

Try a "Letter From Above" on a regular basis. Reread your letters to keep the positive thoughts flowing. Over time, you will be able to track changes and growth.

Questions to Ask Yourself

Here are examples of questions to ask your intuition concerning your life's purpose and goals:

- What is my highest purpose in life?

- What are the obstacles that prevent me from attaining my highest potential?

- How can I fulfill my dreams?

- Is (Plan A) right for me?

- What is the best time for me to implement (Plan A)?

- Where can I find the help and support I need to realize (Plan A/my goals)?

Chapter Eleven

Prosperity

USING THE INTUITION TO MAKE INVESTMENT DECISIONS IS more widespread than you might think. Numerous articles have been published in which brokers, financial planners, and business executives—most of whom wish to remain anonymous—reveal that they consult psychics, dreams, and intuition as aids in making their decisions.

I know many such people myself, financial experts and novices. After realizing the power of his intuition, Brian, a financial novice, decided to try using it to make money in the stock market. For three months, he did nothing but study the market. Then he set goals. Every day, he did intuitive exercises to obtain guidance. Within a year he had made enough money to buy his dream vacation home at the beach.

It was not an entirely smooth ride, however; there were losses as well as gains. "I feel that my intuition made a crucial difference," Brian said. "Without it, I think my dream home would still be a dream instead of a reality."

Intuitive investing is a practice with a successful history. For example, the American tycoon Cornelius Vanderbilt made a profit in gold shortly after the Civil War by consulting spirit guides for advice.

Vanderbilt wanted to capitalize on a fight for control of the gold market. In 1869, he consulted a medium, Victoria Woodhull, whose spirit guides told him to buy gold at one hundred thirty-two dollars an ounce. Already a wealthy man, Vanderbilt followed the advice and invested $9.5 million. Speculation drove the price of gold up. Who knew where it would stop? Vanderbilt knew that when a market is overheated by speculation, the price can plunge as rapidly as it can rise. To make the biggest profit, you have to know the right moment to bail out.

Woodhull told him she had a vision of the number 151, along with a gold bubble bursting. Vanderbilt sold at one hundred and fifty dollars an ounce, making $1.3 million in profits. The price of gold then plummeted.

Please be advised: as in all investments, do not jeopardize your financial security by putting at risk your entire savings. The exercises discussed here are for purposes of experimentation. None is risk free. Results may vary considerably. Remember that intuition shows a probable future based on forces in motion. Markets are volatile, responding to many forces in motion and streams of consciousness.

KNOWLEDGE PLUS INTUITION

It is possible to get intuitive hits about investments without any knowledge of the markets. But if you are serious about intuitive investing, it is imperative that you also educate yourself about the marketplace. Information is the raw material of intuition. The intuition is an organizer of information and insight in bold, new ways. Successful financial planners and brokers are by nature intuitive, whether they realize it or not. They develop their own personal mechanisms for sensing deals, trends, and timing.

To begin, make your commitment and tell your intuitive mind that you wish it to present you with investment advice. Set specific goals. What do you wish to accomplish and in what time frame? Put your commitment and goals in motion with meditation, with affirmations, and as dream incubation instructions. Make a commitment also to act on your guidance, just as you do in other matters in life. What are you willing to do to help realize these goals? You might vow to spend a certain amount of time each day attending to your finances, or to increase your capacity for risk taking.

GETTING THE RIGHT INFORMATION

Intuitive consultant Nancy Rosanoff recommends to "gather information intuitively" and "gather intuitive information." Use your intuition to increase your knowledge of the field. It's important to familiarize yourself with the language and landscape of investing. Let your intuition guide you to the sources right for you. Then, use your intuition to help you make decisions from your knowledge.

Brian, mentioned at the beginning of this chapter, devoted three months to study before making a single investment. During his "intuitive apprenticeship," he made practice investments (no actual money) and then tracked his results. This enabled Brian, a conservative man, to gain confidence in his intuitive investing abilities and sharpen his skill without putting any of his funds at risk.

You may wish to do the same—or you may feel comfortable to learn as you go.

Select any of the exercises in this book to help you frame questions and explore the financial territory. You may discover that information starts coming to you in dreams. Nurture this source by paying more attention to your dreams and asking yourself questions for your dreams to answer.

DISPEL FEAR

Sometimes intuition runs counter to prevailing wisdom and trends. You might receive guidance to sell when everyone else is still buying, such as what happened to Cornelius Vanderbilt. Or you might feel strongly about buying when there is no concrete evidence that a particular stock is going to perform well. Only your experience over time will teach you how to heed your guidance.

Beware of fear. Investing is not for the fearful under any circumstances. Fear colors the intuition and leads to disastrous choices. You can head off fear by practicing detachment from results. Affirm every day that you invest with confidence.

In the exercises for Meditation Adventures, you learned how to remain detached from thoughts, and how to release thoughts as they arise. Practice this with fear as well. If you feel yourself in the grip of fear, gently release it and replace it with light.

If you make a mistake, review how it happened and what you can learn from it and move forward.

ASSOCIATIVE REMOTE VIEWING

As part of your intuitive investment exploration, you might want to try an exercise called "associative remote viewing," so named in parapsychological research. It requires at least three persons and can be done as a group project. Perhaps you are in an investment club or circle that might like to give it a try.

Associative remote viewing is looking into the future for specific events by association. The procedure was developed by researchers Russell Targ, Stephan Schwartz, and Ed May. It works like this:

Simple objects such as a ball or piece of fruit are assigned to several possible future events. For example, the project involves Stock A. A ball represents buy, a stick represents sell, a briefcase represents hold. One person serves as the viewer, who does *not* know either the project or the chosen objects. The viewer looks into the future to see which object will be placed in his hands or presented to him on a certain date. Let's say the viewer looks ahead one month and sees a stick, or an object that is sticklike. The viewer reports his results to an interviewer, who also does not know the particulars of the project or the objects. It is important that both viewer and interviewer do not subconsciously interpret results.

The interviewer reports his findings to the group, which then knows when will be an optimum time to sell Stock A.

Does it work? Results with controlled experiments have varied.

In 1982, the researchers conducted a now-famous associative remote viewing experiment with a renowned remote viewer, Keith Harary, on the silver futures market. A group of anonymous investors bought and sold futures according to the objects perceived by Harary, who did not know what they were. The objects included a vial of perfume, a pair of eyeglass frames, and a plastic bag of washers. More than $100,000 profit was made.

The group fell apart and some litigation resulted. The next year, a subsequent experiment to replicate the results failed. Years later, Targ tried another replication with others and succeeded, but without profit.

THE SPIRITUALITY OF MONEY

The researchers are not the only ones who experience hit-and-miss results when it comes to intuition, the psychic, and money. Many people who have attended workshops and seminars report similar results: intuitive investment can pay off, sometimes handsomely, but can also produce losses. When people make the commitment to stay the course, however, they feel their gains outweigh their losses.

Why is it that our intuition can work spectacularly well except when it comes to money?

One reason has to do with the nature of numbers themselves. As Targ has pointed out, numbers are abstract, and it is often difficult for the intuitive mind to grasp abstracts.

Another reason is, as I pointed out earlier, investing involves the confluence of many minds that are in constant collision.

A major reason has to do with our collective feelings about money. We carry a lot of guilt about wanting money and having money. Our spiritual and religious traditions teach us that desire for money is greed and attachment to the material is "unspiritual."

Spiritual teachers on down through the ages have told us that one must never use spiritual or paranormal powers for personal gain. When one becomes empowered through spiritual study and practice, one should turn to service, not profit.

As a result, we have a schizophrenic discomfort over money. This is particularly evident in the so-called New Age or "spiritual living" arena, where people who wish to earn their living as healers, readers, self-empowerment facilitators, and so on, are criticized for charging fees for their services.

I do not know what the "right" answer is to the philosophical questions about money. Like everything else in life, you must find your own truth and comfort zone about it. Do not let others impose their values on you.

It is our spiritual birthright to be whole and happy and to live to our fullest potential. Our intuition is a natural gift to help us fulfill our birthright. If you wish to use your intuition to increase your wealth, then do so. Whether you use the money for your comfort or for philanthropy is your own private decision.

Questions to Ask Yourself

Set your financial course with the following questions:

- What are the best ways to accomplish my financial goals?

- Is _____the right financial advisor for me?

- When is the best time to _____(buy/sell/hold)?

- Is this the right _____(fund, stock, bond, investment, etc.) for me?

- Should I _____now?

- Where can I find the best sources of data/information that I need?

Chapter Twelve

Improving Your Relationships

YOUR INTUITION WILL HELP YOU BUILD AND MAINTAIN BET-
ter relationships at home, work, social life, and daily life. If you
are not getting along well with someone, your intuition can tell
you why and what to do about it—even the best time to take
action. It will help you find ways to build trust and cooperation,
and deepen intimacy. It will help you zero in on the best business
prospects and sources of help.

EXERCISE #1: MAKING THE MOST OF GATHERINGS AND EVENTS

When I attend a social gathering, I first set a goal. If it's
business oriented, my goal might be to meet the right person(s)
for a project, or to gain the support or interest of someone in
particular. If it's a purely social event, my goal might simply be
to meet a person knowledgeable about a certain subject, or a person with whom I can form a mutually prosperous and fulfilling
friendship. Or, I might want to just enjoy myself without having
to get caught up in someone else's problems.

It's very important to enter a gathering with a purpose set in your intuitive mind. Otherwise, you will be at the mercy of other people's intents. And some of them may have nothing more in mind than aimlessly passing their time—and wasting yours.

For example, I attended a networking event of authors, freelance writers, editors, and others in publishing. My goal: to meet an editor who will buy an idea I wish to write about. Many of the people were strangers to me.

I asked my intuition to show me the person, or persons, whom I should approach to accomplish my goal. As I cast my eye around the room, I was strongly drawn to a woman not far from me. I heard the words "that one" in my inner ear, accompanied by a confirming sensation in the solar plexus.

I made an opportunity to introduce myself. I didn't jump on her with my idea, but got around to it in the course of talking about her magazine and my interests. "Isn't that amazing," she said. "I happen to be looking for someone right now who can write about . . ." What a "coincidence"! I made an appointment to follow up and two weeks later I had a deal.

Perhaps I would have met her sooner or later, but in a large room full of people, I might have spent the entire evening talking to many people, but not the "right" ones.

You can use your intuition in similar circumstances to identify sales prospects, influential persons, news sources, financial sources, and so on—even people to avoid.

Prior to an event, make a clear statement about your goal: what do you wish to leave the event having accomplished?

Ask your intuition to give you an unmistakable sign to help you navigate through the crowd and find the people you need to accomplish your goal.

Give thanks for your success.

EXERCISE #2: FINDING A PARTNER

All of us face the prospect of finding a partner we feel is right for us in every way. Some of us only have to search once; most of us must look again and again as a change of heart, divorce, or loss create new circumstances for us. Your intuition can help you in the search for your ideal partner, or soul mate—someone who matches your emotional, physical, intellectual, and spiritual needs.

Using intuitive free association, compose a portrait of your ideal partner. List the traits, qualities, and characteristics you desire. In another list, state how you would complement or meet those attributes. List everything about you that you would bring to a new relationship.

Now turn your intuition into a beacon or searchlight that will help you find this person.

Everything in the universe is energy. The energy can assume any form and become organized into patterns, such as the physical realm. Matter is energy. Consciousness is energy. Our thoughts and feelings are energy. Creativity is energy. The essence of the soul is energy.

The energies of the universe are in constant motion and interplay. As energies affect each other, they change form. In this fashion, our "reality" is created. W are cocreators of our reality, making it and changing it by what we think, say, and do.

The universe is a mighty current of energy that represents the whole. It constantly moves toward a state of perfection, which is harmony and balance of the whole. Soul mates are an expression of that harmony, balance, and wholeness.

The following exercise will set the intention with your intuitive mind to be in a "perfect flow" and draw to you the circumstances in which you will meet your new partner:

THE GOLDEN STREAM

Imagine yourself floating down a gentle river. Notice that the water is golden. The sunlight falling upon it makes the surface sparkle like millions of golden gems. You are warm, happy, and content, floating easily down the river. You are fully present to the moment. There is no past, no tomorrow, only the eternal moment.

The gems sparkle and flash. The river of water becomes a river of light.

As you float along in the river of light, become aware of your body. It begins to change. See yourself being filled by the golden light of the sun and by the sparkles from the river. The light transforms you, turning you into a golden being. You become lighter and lighter. You see that the golden light that is now you is actually comprised of millions of sparkling golden gem lights, just like the sunlight dancing on the water of the river. Allow yourself to sink deeper and deeper into this field of sparkling lights. You feel energized. Suddenly you realize that you are one and the same with the river of light.

Feel the flow of the motion of light. Allow yourself to be carried along with it. You are filled with complete peace and harmony, at one with the light.

Up ahead you see a round, golden ball of light. It is the Source of All Being, the supply of universal good. The river of light is flowing into it. A cosmic river merging into a cosmic sun. The golden sun is your desire—your union with your ideal partner. The river flows effortlessly into it, merging perfectly with it.

Feel yourself merging with the energy of your partner. It becomes part of you, and you become part of it. You cannot be separated from it. Stay in this space for a few moments and notice how you feel.

When you feel ready, return to an awareness of your physical body. As you feel more solid, know that the light remains within you—the connection to all which is yours.

Questions to Ask Yourself

Your intuition will come to your aid for any matter in a relationship. Whether it's a problem at home or a problem at work, your intuition can help to set things on a smoother course. Are you in a confrontation? Your intuition instantly will tell you what to say or do to defuse the situation.

Your intuition can also tell you where or how to find a new partner, and whether a romantic relationship is on the right course. It's not uncommon to project desires onto relationships. Your intuition will keep you clear-eyed and levelheaded.

Using any of the techniques in this book, ask your intuition to help you with questions such as these:

- What is the reason for the problem with _____?

- How can I resolve my difference with _____?

- When is the best time to _____? (Ask my boss for a raise, discuss a matter, ask for a favor, etc.)

- How can I _____? (Improve my relationship with someone, get better cooperation, get approval for a project, etc.)

- Is my relationship with _____ right for me?

- How can I find the partner who is right for me?

- Where can I find the partner who is right for me?

- Will this relationship _____ (survive/end/change, etc.)?

- How can I motivate _____ to _____?

- What should I say now?

- How can I help _____ with _____?

Chapter Thirteen

Enhancing Your Creativity, Health, and Self-Improvement

ONCE IT IS ENCOURAGED TO BLOSSOM, YOUR INTUITION WILL be a constant source of inspiration and creativity, from ways to make daily life better to ways to change direction in life.

Pay special attention to your ideas, no matter how far-fetched they seem, and keep a record of them. Every idea actually is a glimpse of a real future—one that you have the power to manifest, provided your faith and efforts stay on course. When we let good ideas die out of lack of action, we let our future die with them. Inspired ideas are gifts of the intuition—a vision of a future that can be yours.

Here are some exercises I've found useful in my own life. In particular, "A Pen in the Hand of God" and "Walking the Labyrinth" can be done again and again and always yield fresh treasures.

EXERCISE #1: A PEN IN THE HAND OF GOD

One morning, I sat down in my room to meditate and pray as part of my custom of opening the day's activities. I had a visionary experience that resulted in this exercise that establishes a connection to a divine source of inspiration.

Play some gentle meditation music in the background. Allow the music to relax you. Now read the following text out loud in a slow and measured voice. Or, as an alternative, record the text at an earlier time. For the meditation, play the music and text together, and close your eyes while you listen.

I am a pen in the hand of God.

I stand in the Temple of Eternal Light. Before me is the Book of Life.

The Book of Life is the record of everything that a soul thinks, says, and does. All impulses and acts of consciousness stand written in its pages forever. My acts of compassion. My unkind words. My generosity. My selfishness. My love. My anger. My happiness. My sadness. And so it goes.

I look at the Book of Life. It shimmers gold and white. Its numberless pages go back to before time began and extend into infinite timelessness.

The Book of Life is tended by angels who are the record keepers of the soul's journey to God. They tend to the book without prejudice, without judgment, but with love. They serve God, and they serve the soul in its quest to unite with God. The angels sing constant praises to God. They sing encouragement to the souls who are the living expressions of God.

The angels show me that there are no mistakes in the Book of Life. Only lessons. Some lessons are easy. Some are hard. Sometimes many chapters are written before a single lesson is learned.

What will I write in the Book of Life today? I am a pen in the hand of God.

Will I write that I act out of love? Or will I write that I act out of thoughtlessness?

Thoughtlessness keeps me separated from God. Love brings me into Oneness with God.

Before I write in the Book of Life today, I ask:

What does God wish to write?

The answer arises within my heart:

"Bring Truth, Beauty, Harmony and Love into the world."

I am a pen in the hand of God.

Now write in your journal. Write quickly and without judgment—words, ideas, inspirational pieces, poetry, letters to friends and loved ones, personal feelings—whatever seeks expression.

I do A Pen in the Hand of God at least once a week. It's wonderful for tapping a fresh vein of creativity and for maintaining spiritual balance.

EXERCISE #2: THE INNER ALARM

Your intuition is a watchdog who never sleeps, whose vision is not limited by distance. You can instruct your intuition to watch out for the well-being of anyone or anything. This exercise was inspired by the experience of Harold Sherman, one of the early pioneers of ESP research.

One night Sherman and his wife entertained dinner guests at their New York City apartment. When the guests left, they discovered that thieves had broken into their automobile and stolen some new clothing.

That night Sherman meditated on this. He gave his intuition these instructions: *No one ever will attempt to steal anything of mine but that I will be made aware of the theft in time to prevent it!* He repeated this affirmation until he felt it take hold within his subconscious. He then released it from his conscious mind.

A year later, Sherman met a friend at a restaurant for dinner in New York. He hung his plain, gray overcoat on an open rack and took a table about fifty feet away. He was engaged in an animated conversation when suddenly his inner voice said, *"Quick! That man has your overcoat!"*

> I looked toward the coatrack just as a man had taken a coat from it and was putting it on as he headed toward the cashier's desk. There were perhaps twenty coats on the rack and a number of them, at that distance, looked as though they could have been mine. But now, trained to follow my hunches, I found myself on my feet, cutting through between the tables. En route, my Conscious Mind began to get its licks at me. "Be careful!" it warned. "If you accuse this man of taking your overcoat, and he doesn't have it, you can get yourself in trouble!"
>
> I weighed this warning against my inner feeling and my inner feeling won out.[1]

Sherman informed the man that he had taken his coat. The man vehemently denied it. Fortunately, Sherman had papers in his coat pockets that positively identified him as the owner of the coat. The man apologized and handed him back his coat, saying that it looked like his own. The man took a few steps as though to return to the coatrack and then bolted out the door. Clearly, he had intended to steal the coat.

Note how Sherman paid attention to his intuition twice. The first time came when he had the sudden impression that the man had taken his coat. Then his rational mind interfered, suggesting that it might be a mistake. Sherman did not allow this to overrule his intuition.

Also note that once Sherman had given the watchdog instructions to his intuition, they stayed in force even though a long time had elapsed before they were needed. And, Sherman didn't have the slightest worry about the safety of his overcoat when he met his friend for dinner. Yet he received a warning loud and clear as soon as a situation violated his instructions to his intuition. This demonstrates the incredible power of the intuition to serve us in times of need or an emergency.

Sherman stressed that it is very important to give ourselves the correct instructions, otherwise we will get the wrong result. Instructions, or affirmations, should be worded to reflect the results we desire, not the results we fear. Said Sherman:

> If I had feared that I would, someday, be the victim of a
> theft, and had I strongly pictured this possibility, this would
> have been the same as ordering my higher faculties of mind
> to create a susceptibility in me for such a happening. Under
> such conditions, it is not likely that my mind would have re-
> acted in a way to protect me, as it so obviously did in confor-
> mance with my prior instruction.[2]

How would you like your intuition to be your all-seeing watchdog for you? We know from our exercises in expanded vision, expanded listing, and remote viewing that our consciousness can be sent to distant locations. You can ask your intuition to protect your premises while you are away, guard your house while you sleep, watch your belongings, and protect you while you travel. This does not mean, of course, that you are then free to be careless or take unnecessary risks. But your intuition will be like an extra insurance policy.

Here are some affirmation instructions to activate your inner alarm, including the example given by Sherman:

- No one will ever attempt to steal anything of mine but that I will be made aware of the theft in time to prevent it

- If anyone attempts to break into my home or property, I will know it in time to prevent it

- I will be alerted to any unsafe conditions in my travel in time to avoid them

- I will be alerted to any threats to my personal safety in time to avoid them

In a meditative state, repeat one of these affirmations—or one you write to suit your specific needs—until you feel it is "locked" into consciousness. Sherman, who was very experienced using his psyche and intuitive faculties, programmed his intuition once. I find it useful to periodically refresh an affirmation.

EXERCISE #3: WALKING THE LABYRINTH

The labyrinth is a walking meditation revered since ancient times for its transformative and healing powers. It is an archetypal mandala for a journey of consciousness, a search for knowledge and truth. Laid out on the ground or a floor, the labyrinth is entered and walked in a circular fashion to its center, and then exited by another circular route. When we walk the labyrinth, we experience a quieting of the mind, an opening of the heart, and an awakening of wholeness, oneness, and potential. The labyrinth inspires change from within a deep level of the self. We experience a refreshing renewal that leads to peace of mind and clarity of thoughts. We experience intuitive flashes and breakthroughs.

The motif of the labyrinth has appeared for thousands of years in mythology, architecture, art, dance, rites, and rituals. The oldest surviving labyrinth, dating to c. 2500 B.C.E., appears on a rock carving at Luzzanas on the island of Sardinia, Italy. Fragments of labyrinth designs can be traced back to 6500 B.C.E. The Egyptians, Greeks, Celts, and Indians made great use of them.

The term "labyrinth" is believed to come from *labrys,* or the double axe, a symbol of the Greek god Zeus. The double axe was the symbol of power in the Minoan culture of ancient Crete, where labyrinths were especially prevalent.

In the Middle Ages, the labyrinth became a walking substitute for the sacred pilgrimage to the Holy Land. During the wars of the Crusades, from the eleventh to thirteenth centuries, journeys to the Holy Land were dangerous. The Roman Catholic Church designated seven cathedral labyrinths in Europe as acceptable replacements that would offer the same spiritual renewal as an actual pilgrimage. Walking the labyrinth gave pilgrims the experience of communion with the ultimate reality: the knowledge of Self, and the knowledge that God and Self are one. The most famous labyrinth still remaining is on the floor of the cathedral at Chartres, France.

When the Renaissance ushered in the Age of Science, labyrinths began to decline in importance. They faded from spiritual practice. In recent years, the labyrinth has been revived and greeted with tremendous enthusiasm as people once again have connected with the power of the path. In the United States, the Reverend Dr. Lauren Artress, Cannon of Special Ministries at Grace Cathedral Church in San Francisco and author of *Walking the Sacred Path*, created a labyrinth at her church that has drawn more than one million visitors from all over the world. Artress describes the labyrinth's path as a metaphor for our own spiritual journey: all you have to do is follow the path, and it will take you inward.

Artress's work has inspired the construction of labyrinths in numerous other locations: in parks, at hospitals, on company grounds. Labyrinth workshops are popular. Even healing has been ascribed to them: patients with severe or catastrophic illness report improvements after walking the labyrinth.

The labyrinth has no dead ends and wrong turns, but has one path that leads to the center. Thus it represents the mystery of the soul's journey to the Mystic Center. The path does not go directly to the center, but takes a meandering, circular route that enables the traveler to go through distinct shifts in consciousness along the way. From the center, the same path leads out. This represents the return to the world, in which the gifts of illumination are brought back to be manifested in life.

The labyrinth symbolizes the journey of regeneration and enlightenment found in many religious traditions. In Christianity, this journey is called Union with God. In Buddhism, it is the Path to Enlightenment, and in Hinduism, the Path to Freedom.

You can find the nearest labyrinths to you by doing a search on the Internet. Since it is not always possible—or convenient—to visit one, here is an alternative: the portable finger labyrinth, a simplified version of the one at Chartres. The route is "walked" with a finger, pencil, or colored pen. It can be just as effective as physically walking a full-size labyrinth. The key is your intent.

You will find a finger labyrinth in Appendix A.

IN PREPARATION FOR THE LABYRINTH, COMPOSE A QUESTION to which you seek an answer. Address a significant matter. Be willing to accept whatever answers arise from your experience.

THERE ARE THREE STAGES TO WALKING THE LABYRINTH:

Stage 1: Entering the labyrinth. As you walk to the center, focus on the releasing, emptying, and quieting of negative thoughts. Relinquish the things you have sought to control and the worries that control you, and surrender yourself to the journey. If annoying thoughts keep intruding, gently release them—do not try to resist them or dismiss them. Travel the path slowly. Have no expectations—only an open mind and an open heart ready to receive the gifts of the labyrinth.

In mystical terms, this stage is called Purgation, which is the release of all things that block communication with our Higher Self. We cannot hear the inner voice when our minds are busy.

Stage 2: Entering the center. Many times reaching the center of the labyrinth comes as a surprise because of the winding, circular path. You don't know you're "there" until you're there—which reflects what oftentimes happens in life. The key to realizing life's potential is to be present to the moment. Only when we are present to the moment are we in contact with our full creative potential.

Once in the center of the labyrinth, linger for a moment, for it is here that breakthroughs in intuition and creativity occur. The gifts of the labyrinth reveal themselves in startling clarity. They may include insight into a problem or situation; new perspectives; creative ideas; and feelings of empowerment, integration, receptivity, authenticity, and self-confidence.

In mystical terms, this stage is called Illumination, which is the knowing of the sacred Self within.

Stage 3: Leaving the labyrinth. On the journey out, allow yourself to feel replenished, balanced, and empowered by your experience. Travel slowly to allow the new energies to take hold. Be absorbed in your self-revelation.

In mystical terms, this stage is called Union, which means communion with and being absorbed in God. We bring Truth into our being.

Following exit from the labyrinth, spend some quiet time in meditation and reflection to integrate the experience. Record your experience and insights in your journal.

Your experiences with the labyrinth will vary. Sometimes they will be profound. Other times you might simply feel relaxed. "Walking the Labyrinth" is an alchemical process that continues to unfold. Like other forms of innerwork, the labyrinth opens one up to new flows of energies. Pay attention to dreams and synchronicities, which can bring more intuitive information, wisdom, and ideas. Daily prayer and meditation also augment the labyrinth experience.[3]

YOUR INNER HEALTH ADVISOR

Your Higher Self intuitively knows how to keep you balanced and centered. Many times we don't pay attention and indulge in bad habits that affect our health: not enough sleep, wrong food, too much stress, too little exercise, and so on. Remedies to our well-being may seem obvious, but let's face it: we often look straight past the obvious.

Make it your daily habit to meditate. Meditation—as well as prayer and contemplation—can greatly reduce stress, one of the major factors behind many of our health problems.

Instruct your intuition to help you enhance and maintain health and well-being. Janice could barely make it through a day without her energy flagging. She often found it hard to concentrate; sometimes she was easily irritated. She knew she was trying to juggle too much, but felt she had to maintain her activities. When she asked her inner health advisor for help, she received a mental impression of herself asleep. At first she thought it was a joke—her Higher Self telling her she was asleep at the wheel of life. The guidance clarified with these words: "Get more sleep."

An obvious answer, but impossible, Janice thought. In fact, she was thinking of cutting back on her nightly sleep in order to compensate for her lethargy during the day. She could accomplish a lot with an extra thirty minutes a day.

The inner guidance was insistent: "Get more sleep." She had the "feeling" that she really needed about an hour more than she was allowing herself. Losing an hour seemed unthinkable.

Janice finally decided to follow the guidance. She had no trouble at all sleeping an extra hour each night—her body seemed to drink up the additional sleep. She quickly realized an improvement in her well-being: in mood, energy, concentration, and vitality. To her surprise, she discovered that she was able to get more done in less time during the day. "I made the mistake of being ruled by statistics," she said. "I slept according to what I understood was 'average.' The truth is, I seem to need more sleep than most others. My intuition called my attention to what my body was already trying to tell me."

Some years ago, I received a strong inner prompting to cut back on my exposure to daily news. I was in the habit of watching news shows in the morning, evening and prior to bed—plus whenever I happened to plunk down on the couch for a break from work.

Daily news is overwhelmingly bad: accidents, murders, political tension, scandals, disasters, unhappy people. While it behooves us to stay reasonably informed about important events and developments, we simply do not need to know all the bad news that happens around the planet every day. Most of these events are beyond our control and sphere of influence. But listening to accounts of them drains us emotionally. These negative effects can stay with us for a long time.

I found that when I cut back substantially on television news shows, I experienced an overall lifting of stress and tension. I did not feel that I was in the dark. I turned to newspapers and news magazines (and now the Internet), where I can control what I want to know and when.

A couple of years after I implemented this habit, I read Dr. Andrew Weil's book, *Spontaneous Healing*, and was delighted to find a confirming viewpoint. Weil recommended periodic "news fasts" as part of an overall good health program. He observed:

> By the way, a major source of my own mental turmoil is the news. The percentage of stories in the news that make me feel good is very small; the percentage of stories that make me feel anxious or outraged is very large and increasing, as news media focus more and more on murder, mayhem, and misery. It is easy to forget that we have a choice as to whether we let this information into our minds and thoughts.[4]

How else does our intuition help us with health?

Our intuition often gives us early warnings and advice about health matters. I have studied dreams for most of my life and have found dreams to be an especially rich source of this kind of information. The diagnostic and healing power of dreams has been known and used since ancient times around the world. Sometimes illness is forecast in dreams before obvious symptoms show up in the body. And, when we are injured or ailing, dreams sometimes help us with information that speeds our recovery. By paying attention to our dreams, we receive intuitive guidance that can help us to maintain good health.

In *The Power of the Mind to Heal*, Joan Borysenko recounts how dreams alerted her to a precancerous condition in her breast. In her dream, she was clutching a bottle of nitroglycerin over her right breast. She arrived at the hospital just in time for a nurse to throw the nitroglycerin down the drain before it could explode. When she awakened, she could still feel a sensation of heat in her breast. After more breast dreams, she said, "I believed that the unconscious wisdom of the body might be trying to give me an important message."

Borysenko visited a doctor, who was skeptical that anything was wrong. She had no obvious lumps and her mammograms were clear except for a small calcium deposit. The doctor dismissed the dream and suggested she find a way to manage anxiety and cancer phobia.

Months later, reminded of the nitroglycerin dreams, Borysenko had the calcium deposit biopsied. It was diagnosed as precancerous and not yet malignant. She was relieved. "The 'nitroglycerin' was poured down the drain before it could explode," she said.[5]

Experiences such as this are well documented in medical, psychotherapy, dream and self-help literature.[6]

Our intuition uses other ways to reach us about our health besides dreams. For example, in *I Bring You Glad Tidings*, I tell the story of a young man who discovered his own cancer after hearing a friend tell him about the same kind of cancer that had struck the friend's mother. The cancer was in the neck. As he heard the story, the young man felt an urge to rub his own neck—and felt a suspicious lump.[7]

If your intuition tugs at you concerning your health, pay attention. But please note: the intuition is not a substitute for medical diagnosis or treatment or other professional health care.

Questions to Ask Yourself

Here are questions to pose concerning your creativity, health and self-improvement:

- How can I better develop my talent for _____?

- What new talents should I explore?

- How can I increase my happiness and satisfaction in life?

- How should I improve/change my lifestyle?

- How can I heal _____?

- How can I lose weight and keep it off?

- How can I _____(overcome bad habits, change behavior, etc.)?

Chapter Fourteen

Achieving Abundant Living

PERHAPS YOUR INTEREST IN INTUITION STARTED WITH A DE-sire to make better decisions. Your intuition will do that for you, but it will do much more. Your intuition will make possible more abundant living. It will help you reach your goals and make your dreams come true.

I'd like to share a few final thoughts on happiness, fulfillment, and abundant living.

Master Affirmations

Your self-improvement plan should include the regular use of affirmations, which help to condition your intuition—as well as your beliefs, thoughts and actions—to respond in desired ways. If you have been working with affirmations as part of the devel-opment plan set forth in this book, then you have already expe-rienced their power to facilitate transformation and break-throughs.

I'm a fan of the hugely popular comic strip *Dilbert*, centered around a hapless engineer at the mercy of a dehumanized workplace. When a business executive friend of mine told me that Dilbert's creator, Scott Adams, had used affirmations to build his success, naturally I was intrigued. Scott's experiences are in his book, *The Dilbert Future: Thriving on Business Stupidity in the 21st Century*.

According to Scott, he tried affirmations on the recommendation of a friend. He neither believed in them nor disbelieved in them. He did not feel that they required any particular faith or positive thinking to work. He picked what he thought was a "very unlikely goal" and went to work on it, writing his affirmation fifteen times a day and visualizing it. Within a week, he experienced strings of amazing coincidences, and, within a few months, the goal was accomplished.

He then tried an affirmation to "get rich in the stock market." He wrote the affirmation and waited for inspiration. One morning he awakened at 4 A.M. with the words "buy Chrysler" in his mind. The intuition came on the brink of a spectacular recovery of Chrysler stock (Scott did not buy the stock, however, due to difficulties in getting a brokerage account established).

He tried again with stocks and received another accurate intuition about a company just going public, whose stock climbed rapidly. Scott made a small profit—the stock continued to rise after he sold it. (I suspect that his experiences would have had a greater return if he had devoted some intent to studying the market.)

Scott turned affirmations toward other goals, all of which were successful. For example, he scored a ninety-fourth percentile on his exam to qualify for a master of business administration program. He became a successful syndicated cartoonist despite enormous odds against him. He turned *Dilbert* into "the most successful comic on the planet," realizing that goal when two of his *Dilbert* books rode to the top of the *New York Times* bestseller list.

It's an interesting account. However, I firmly believe that faith and positive thinking are intrinsic to the success of affirmations. Affirmations do focus your intent and consciousness whether you are aware of it or not. Faith and positive thinking—and thus action—are conditioned in the process. If your commitment to a goal is vague or filled with doubt, affirmations are not likely to be successful.

I have used affirmations in all areas of life: relationships, health, success, creativity, and my spiritual path. They are wonderful tools for strengthening vision, determination, and perseverence, especially when energy flags and faith droops.

I always phrase my affirmations in the present tense: "I am . . ." "I have . . ." "I receive . . ." This creates the expectation that the goal is already obtained.

Remember to follow the five-step advice given in Chapter 4:

1. Create a clear affirmation

2. Believe in every cell of your being that it is right for you

3. See yourself as having achieved or attained your goal now

4. Ask for guidance and help through your intuition

5. Do everything you can to create your new reality

Don't overload your intuition with too many affirmations at a time. Select two or three to work with over a period of a few months.

Here are twenty-two master affirmations that will enhance your self-confidence, self-empowerment, creativity, relationships, health and well-being, financial prosperity, and decision-making ability:

- I honor and use my special abilities and skills

- I have a unique and special contribution to make

- I accept prosperity and abundance into my life

- I trust that everything comes at perfect time and in the perfect way

- I am open to receive with every breath that I take

- I am peaceful, relaxed, and centered

- I trust myself

- I am lovable and loving

- I am beautiful and radiant

- I am enjoying health and energy

- I am the master of my life

- I am whole and complete in myself

- I am in radiant health, filled with light and love

- I am happy and satisfied in my relationship with (name)

- I enjoy great financial prosperity

- I express original, creative ideas

- I make the right decisions

- I have plenty of energy for all that I choose to do

- I am beautiful, loving, and lovable

- I appreciate my body

- I am relaxed and centered

- I receive infinite riches that are now flowing freely into my life

MEDITATION EXERCISES FOR AFFIRMATIONS

Use meditative visualization exercises to help the manifestation of your affirmations.

Select an affirmation for prosperous living. Follow the procedures for intuitive breathing and relaxation.

When you are ready, repeat the affirmation either aloud or silently. As you do so, build a vivid mental image of the affirmation. Let yourself star in it. Activate all your senses in the imagery. Make the picture as intense and vivid as possible.

Hold the image as long as you can.

Release the image. As you release it, give thanks for its manifestation in your life. Give thanks for having what you envision *now*.

Carry the image with you in your thoughts. Call it up often.

If you feel doubt, then examine why. Perhaps you don't feel you deserve what you seek. You must get to the root cause and correct it. Perhaps you need to reword the affirmation, or work with another one first.

KEEP A RECORD OF YOUR PROGRESS WITH AFFIRMATIONS. *Expect* results—you will get them!

Living Intuitively and Abundantly

Connie Bowen is a talented artist and author of empowering children's books: *I Believe in Me* and *I Turn to the Light: A Book of Healing Affirmations*. When I met Connie, she shared with me the unfoldment of her life's path and creativity—all the results of paying heed to God's guidance spoken through her inner voice,

252 ROSEMARY ELLEN GUILEY

which she calls her spirit guides, and through dreams. A deeply spiritual woman, she is firmly connected to her intuition. Her success and personal fulfillment are testimony to the fruits of following one's guidance. She was led naturally to do many of the things discussed in this book.

Connie's intuitive guidance opened in response to deep yearnings for fulfillment of her highest purpose. In the beginning, she didn't even know what that purpose was, much less how she would achieve it. But she asked a question, and an answer was given. She paid attention.

Connie was in her early thirties, married with no children, living near Portland, Oregon, and working full-time as a court reporter. Life was stable, but Connie felt that something vital was missing. She explained:

> For years I had felt empty. I would drive down the highway and take a deposition, drive back home and transcribe it, and drive back downtown to deliver it. That was my life. One day I put down my briefcase in my driveway and looked up at the stars and said, "Is this it? Is the epitaph on my tombstone going to say, 'She got her transcripts out on time. She made all her deadlines.'?" I felt that this was my only achievement for this life—always on time with my transcripts.
>
> A little voice came to me and said, "First you will have a child, and then your life will change." That was a shock! I immediately wanted to know how my life would change. Would I be a teacher? I couldn't imagine it. There were no children in my life. I wasn't involved with them. But there was no further information given—that was it.

And so the door was opened. As is often the case, guidance is brief and cryptic. There is no full explanation of the how's and when's to assure us that anything at all will come to pass. This is the point where many of us stop. We are afraid to budge without guarantees, time lines, safety nets, and knowing exactly what will happen.

It seldom works that way.

Connie was thirty-three when she and her husband divorced, but remained friends. A major life change propels many people into a spiritual search, and so it did for Connie. She began attending a weekly session on the teachings of *A Course in Miracles*. But the predictions of the inner voice seemed distant. Nonetheless, Connie intuitively felt that she would remarry, and would meet her next husband through the course. She also intuitively felt that she would have a child. But most of the men she dated already had families from previous marriages and were not especially interested in starting new ones. She felt frustrated and fell into what she called a "chasm period." This is the valley between intuition and manifestation: you see the potential, but it remains out of grasp. It is a vulnerable time for many. Doubts can flood into the chasm and threaten to drown faith.

Connie held on to her convictions about remarriage and a child. One day her future husband showed up at a meeting.

> When Michael walked in to our group, a little voice in my mind said, "There he is." I hadn't really been watching everyone, asking "Is he the one, is he the one?" It was more just a quiet knowing. If you open up to these feelings and start to really notice them, you find that they're very apparent all of the time, even about the most minute details of your life.

Connie and Michael married. When she was forty, a son, Matthew was born. The future revealed by the voices was bearing out.

While she was taking the course, Connie had a mystical experience that opened yet another door.

I was sitting on the couch meditating, with my crystals in my lap. I was doing a lot of forgiveness in my meditation. I was repeating the affirmation, "I am a channel for divine light and love," and was feeling very loving and peaceful. My eyes were shut, but up in the right corner of my eye appeared a brilliant circular light. It was pulsating as if it were alive and thinking. I had never seen a light like that. It was not like the sun. It was a brilliant light that penetrates your core.

With my eyes still shut, I said to myself, "What's that?" The light jumped in size. I'm looking at it and can't believe what I'm seeing. It seemed that the light was coming down to me. Then it jumped in size again.

When it did, I left my body through what I later found out was my heart chakra. I went up into this light. A voice in front of me said, "She is afraid." I was literally let go—it was exactly like being released by a magnet—and I snapped back into my body through the heart chakra. I felt myself going back in my body past my heart. My heart made a beat. I knew the power of the universe, or God, the One Source, was beating my heart. That one source pumps everyone's heart. It is very easy for this source to do that.

I felt my mind stretch as far as God's mind could stretch. I was one with God and felt all of this knowledge come into me. I knew so many things instantly because I was one with all knowledge. In that moment, I definitely knew that we live beyond our bodies and that we are more than our bodies. I tell people that when you are in your body, you are a cotton ball, and when you are out of your body, you are a diamond. That's the contrast I experienced.

I felt the serenity, strength, and power of who I really was. It has nothing to do with this body. If all of me were contained in this body, it would explode. So as I came back into my body, I knew that I was a dilution of my total self.

Then I was in kind of a shock. I meditated for a while

more. I went outside into the yard. My former husband was taking things out of the garage. He was standing with his new wife. I'd always thought of them as a total unit—they were so much in love. I saw them now as separate beings, each on their own path. They looked like children to me, even though they were in their midthirties. Their age to me was about six or seven. It would be as though we had a life expectancy of five hundred to six hundred years.

They were such brilliant lights, I just stared at them. It was as though a sun were resident inside their bodies, shining through each pore of their beings so that you would have to squint to see them. It was more than an aura around them— it was as though they were suns. I looked at them and spoke to them, but I was in another reality superimposed on this reality.

I met my former mother-in-law for lunch. I just loved everyone I saw. A waitress came over to take our order, and I looked at her and loved her and felt that she should sit down and have lunch with us and tell us her story. I felt almost a pain that there was a separation between us. There was an aching in my chest, in the heart chakra, all day. The only thing that would help that aching was to hug someone. It made me wonder where the whole idea of hugging came from. I think it has something to do with our heart chakra.

Then I fell into a mild depression for about a year. I was searching for an answer as to why we are in these bodies, when I had felt the magnificence of who we are when we are outside our bodies. Why are we here, what could we possibly be doing in this material world with our bodies? I'd never questioned that before.

Connie's search led to her career as an author. When Matthew was about one year old, she realized that he was old enough to have spiritual ideas presented to him.

I had this idea that I would do some affirmations with drawings to correspond to them that would appeal to a young
child. I was still working full-time as a court reporter. I
didn't realize what I was starting. I wrote down fifty affirmations. I didn't do any market research as to whether this
might be a good idea for a book—I was simply doing something for Matthew. I took a week off work and did the drawings. Once I started the project I found that I could not stop.
It was the weirdest feeling. But there was a negative voice
going on inside my head saying, "What are you doing with
this project? You need to get your transcripts done. You
need to get to work."

That voice is one we all hear when intuition prompts us to a
bold course of action. A part of us seeks to rise up and say no, it
can't be done, we're being foolish, or we should get back to doing
what makes sense. We test our vision. It is another vulnerable
time, and many people give up their visions.

Connie, however, held fast to her vision and continued with
her project. It was validated through synchronicity.

People would come to the house and like the drawings and
affirmations and ask for one for their own children. A friend
suggested I should put them together into a book. I'd done
no research about publishers and what was involved in getting a book published. I thought you did your book and it
came out into the stores two weeks later. I submitted my
material to a publisher suggested by my friend, and I was
very nervous about it.

Months and months went by with no decision from the publisher. Connie's material was being used in a church near her, and
the publisher told her at one point that if someone from the
church would write a letter of recommendation, it would help. A

letter was promised, but months went by and it was not written. The waiting took its toll.

> But I kept getting the guidance to wait for this publisher. The whole time, my ego was saying, "You really ought to try to find another publisher. This is ridiculous." But each time I tried to look up other publishers, it felt so wrong. I finally did contact one, and they rejected the book. I felt so frustrated with the whole process. Here I'd had this intense guidance to do the project, and now I was in that chasm period, where you need a lot of faith.
>
> So, I wrote out in my journal how the book had been published in several languages and was going around the world spreading joy. I wrote my highest expectation for this book: that I had retired from court reporting and was doing art full-time. It was my wildest dream. I wrote it as if it were a newspaper article and the interview was about me and my story. It flowed right out of me so easily. I reread it and reread it 12 times—it made me feel great, as though it all was here already. Tears were streaming down my cheeks, I was so happy.

Two days later, Connie felt a "definite shift" in her consciousness. She received word that the promised letter of recommendation was on its way to the publisher. Soon thereafter, Connie's book was accepted for publication. She had waited for fourteen months and had not given up because her guidance had told her to be patient.

I Believe in Me became one of the publisher's most successful titles. True to Connie's vision, it was translated into foreign languages and published around the world. She was able to quit her court reporting job and work on art and writing full-time.

Connie turned her attention to an idea she had for a second

children's book. The idea had come in a dream during the time of waiting for the decision on the first book.

> The person in the dream was turned toward a circular light. Angels were coming down to the person. The symbolism there was to turn toward the light to remember who you are. It was such a vivid dream.

When I woke up, I told my husband that I wanted to draw it. Then I had this idea that a book that could help lift people up out of depression or grief to remember who they are through pictures and affirmations would be helpful for older children and adults. I did a series of about thirty drawings and did affirmations for those.

After *I Believe in Me* was published, I sent the material to my publisher. While they were considering it, I strengthened my connection to guides, and the affirmations for each drawing changed as a result. For example, for a drawing of a woman holding a ball of light with the sunrise behind her, I had written, "I cultivate the seeds of my awareness. They are precious signs of my awakening." The guides pointed out to me that my favorite affirmations for little ones were composed in simple, powerful statements. They said I should change it to, "I have awakened."

So I argued with them. That's another way I can tell I'm getting higher guidance is if I argue over it. I said, "How can I say I have awakened? If we've awakened, we are ascended masters, and we're no longer here."

They answered, "God could not and would not set before you an arduous journey that you must undertake to being you. This, your God, would not and could not do. Only believe you have found your own sweet nature and let this belief fill the seeming emptiness and longing. Let this belief free to envelope you and guide you. It is only in belief held

long and unquestioning can such a journey be." Thus I understood that we are only unawakened in our perception.

Connie followed her guidance and changed the affirmations.
Another helping hand from the guides came as a simple direction. While Connie was working on her second book, she kept
her ideas for it in her filing cabinet in a folder marked "Book."
One day she heard these words in her head: "If you want more
than one book published, put an 's' on the word book."

The guides also advised, "Work with your expectations. Your
expectations must rise to the level as when you are expecting a
package and you listen for the truck coming by. You have one
ear out for the truck. Once you pray and ask, believe and let your
expectation rise to the level."

Connie let her expectations rise, and the second book was
published as *I Turn to the Light: A Book of Healing Affirmations*.

Initially the book did well, and then sales dipped. Connie
became worried. She asked for a sign about it and was given her
answer in a vivid dream:

> There was an old woman. A large bird was coming to her,
> and she was fighting it off. It was circling around her head
> and bothering her. She was trying to wave the bird off. I said
> to myself in the dream, "Omigosh, it's a vulture!" Suddenly
> the bird landed in front of her. She looked at it again, and it
> was a stork. The dip in sales wasn't a death—it was a birth.
> Later I found out that vultures and storks are part of the
> same family.

Though Connie could ease her concern over the book, she did
continue to be concerned about making ends meet on the uncertain fortunes of book publishing. Few authors make a full-time
living on their craft. Income is often erratic and unpredictable.

I was on a budget, counting pennies. I had a vivid dream
that I had an earthen bowl in my hands. There was a woman
cooking pancakes. I was scooping the batter out of the bowl
with my hands and giving it to her. I scooped out the batter
and gave it to her, and she made the pancakes. The bowl was
somehow filled again. I scooped it out and gave it to her
again. She made the pancakes and the bowl filled up again.
She turned to me and said, "This time give me all the batter." So I scooped it all out and the bowl filled up again from
the inside. A voice very clearly said, "The bowl will never be
empty again."

It was a profound dream for me and still is. Here I was,
scrimping and saving, and I'm being told the bowl will never
be empty again.

After the dream things started to happen. We came into
an inheritance. Whenever I find myself entering into fear, I
remember that dream. Our bowl fills up from the inside:
God is the source.

Years earlier, Connie had simply asked a heartfelt question
about her life, "Is this it?" By following the guidance that opened
as a result of asking the question, her entire life blossomed.

Things have opened up for me since I made the commitment
to go on a different path in my life, to follow my creativity.
My spirit guides have given me reams of information. It
comes through the inner voice. I can tell the difference between that voice and my own. It feels infinitely far away and
yet infinitely close at the same time. It's hard to explain. It's
intimate yet far away. It's very peaceful and there is no emotion associated with the voice. I feel like I receive knowledge
that I already know, and it stays with me in a way that an
ego voice would not. If I'm thinking about an idea and I feel
a certain shift in consciousness, then I know it's coming from

the Higher Self. They are always telling me how we are all one and I can't be separated or lost from my guidance.

Connie is faithful to her journaling, a tool that stimulates the guidance. She writes to herself as though her guardian angel is speaking: "Dear Connie . . ." She also uses an affirmation the guides gave her: "Joy is my compass."

"Joy is my compass" is something that came out of my writing. The guidance was, when working your way through the pros and cons of a situation, let joy be your compass. It helps you through areas of confusion. Always follow the path of joy, the path of self. Once you start to follow that—the path of joy or what is most spiritually nourishing to you—joy will increase. The inner voice will increase. People will come into your life who will support what you are trying to accomplish. Doors will open for you. The path of joy is your core self. Your soul is speaking to you about what you have come here to do—what is most in line with who you are.

I try to stay really in tune with what brings me the most fulfillment. I stay away from the idea of material success. We can be very successful materially but feel very empty. The guides tell me to have trust, to do my work, and not be concerned with the effects. The rest will follow. What we consider success may not be the true purpose of something. For example, success may be helping someone so that they in turn can help someone else. Success in the material world may not be the ultimate purpose of what you do.

The guides have made other points about living spiritually and intuitively:

- Everyone is equal. No one is less miraculous than the other person. That would mean God was picking favorites, and it is impossible for God to pick a favorite. We are like links on a chain—no link above, no link below. When someone has a perception that a person is more blessed than another, they are entering into an illusion. Our choices create what we do and why. We can change it any moment. If you find yourself feeling less than whole, then choose again. There is no judgment. Everything is a learning experience. There are no mistakes. A "mistake," they said, is "but a path chosen in a moment of haste, perhaps, or in answer to the urging of the voice of fear that tells you, you must do this thing in earnest which your heart is not wanting you to do, or go where it is not your heart that has chosen for you." There is no need to carry the anvil of guilt. Let the anvil become ash, light and airy, and float in the wind, and let the guilt dissolve. We learn that we need to come back to an awareness of ourselves.

- It is impossible for God to keep a secret from you. That's why it doesn't feel good when we keep a secret from someone else. Whenever we enter into the illusion of behaving in a manner other than our God self, it is like keeping a secret.

- God is not mysterious. "When you speak of 'His mysterious ways,' we all take quite a chuckle in delight," they said. "For this does show us how 'mysterious' you do find your God to be, and thus yourself. Remember His ways are your ways, His breath of Life is your very breath, and His Love is your very life force within you. We entreat you to turn to God for every supposed need, every question as to which direction to reach for with your very next step, and His mighty arm will carry you when a burden you have laid upon your back."

- Fear holds an empty promise. An empty promise is a promise unfulfilled. Sometimes we're afraid to do something because we might fail, or because of what others might think. Fear promises all day long what might happen if you do this or that. But it's really an empty promise. Choose love instead.

Connie's affirmation for the latter point is, "Fear holds an empty promise. I choose love."

I asked Connie, "After going through this transformation, what do you see now as your epitaph?"

"I would like to tell people, 'Ask for what you need.' I'm always asking for a sign that I'm on the right path. The answer always comes. When it does, you will know beyond the shadow of the doubt that it is the answer you seek. It will come in the right and perfect way for you."

CONNIE'S STORY OF UNFOLDMENT IS BEAUTIFUL—AND IT CAN happen to anyone who makes the decision to listen to his or her guidance and follow it. You have within you a treasure-house of wisdom that will not fail you. Instead of looking to others for direction and advice, look within.

Connie once asked her guides why others sought her out for advice rather than looking within. They said:

> You are a beacon—once you reach the other shore—the shore they are going to, they wish you to throw them a rope. They have yet to realize—they need no rope—for they have wings.

> So spread your wings and fly!

The Labyrinth

Intuition Etiquette

YOU'RE HAVING A CONVERSATION WITH SOMEONE WHEN suddenly you have intuitive impressions about them. You feel the urge to speak up. Should you?

Someone finds out you're "psychic" and comes up to you and asks for a demonstration of your ability. Should you give one?

Someone asks you to see into the future for them. Should you?

It's inevitable that you will be caught off guard in situations such as these unless you give some thought to your "intuition etiquette." It may not always be appropriate to say what you intuit.

Always keep in mind that your intuition is a skill and a tool, not a toy. It should be used wisely. Here are some guidelines for sound intuition habits.

Social Settings

SPEAK BY INVITATION ONLY

In the course of daily interactions with people, you find your-self intuitively aware of emotions or circumstances in their life. Some of them might be troubling. Perhaps you also intuit a so-lution to a problem or an outcome of a stressful situation. In the full blaze of your intuitive glory, you blurt out, "I know you're worried about your daughter taking that trip by herself, but she's going to be fine." Or, "I think you should sell that piece of prop-erty." Or, perhaps you offer a well-intended inspirational boost: "There's no need to be so depressed about your finances—you've got a lot of good things going for you!" Rather than being show-ered with gratitude, you are met with reactions ranging from puzzlement to discomfort to irritation—even anger. Stung, you wonder why. You were only trying to help.

Your heart may have been in the right place, but you unwit-tingly intruded upon the other person's private space. Most people do not appreciate unsolicited advice no matter what the source. The demonstration that you know something personal that has not been broached verbally may also upset someone. While in-tuition has made its way into many public arenas of thought, most people do not like the idea that others, especially casual acquain-tances or strangers, may be able to see into their minds. Some persons may be truly frightened by it as well. At the very least, your advice may go unabsorbed, rolling off like water from a duck's back. Everyone moves through life at their own pace, and your unsolicited comments may be premature.

It's better to keep spontaneous intuitive impressions to your-self. Let them become part of your overall understanding of some-one else. File them away, and if the opportunity presents itself, make use of them when your views are invited.

There are times when exceptions are made to this rule. Speak up if your intuition is strongly telling you to do so. You may be serving as a tool of divine intervention—a synchronicity in which someone hears what they need to hear in order to take action. You must be *very* clear about this, however, for it's all too easy to fall into the glamor that you are a walking tool of divine intervention all the time.

Sometimes our intuitions provide warnings. Leah dreamed that something was wrong with one of the rear wheels of her son's car, and she awoke with the feeling that he shouldn't be driving it. He was about to take a long driving trip—one that she disapproved of. Was the dream a genuine intuitive/psychic message, or a reflection of her feelings about the trip? Because Leah knew the language of her dreams, she recognized her personal intuitive/psychic hallmarks in this one. She took it as a warning to pass on to her son. The car seemed to be in good condition, but a closer inspection revealed that one of the rear wheels was in danger of falling off. If it had done so on the highway, Leah's son may have been killed or seriously injured, or stranded in a remote location.

SPEAK GENTLY

If you do offer your intuitive insights, do so in a soft and agreeable manner easy for another person to accept. Avoid dictatorial statements such as "You must . . ." "You have to . . ." Rather, say "I feel that" or "My impression is that it would be best to . . ." Do not boast that you are infallible or always right. Remember that intuition sees behind the surface into delicate areas and picks up on the probable outcomes of forces in motion. Forces can change, and so can outcomes.

DECLINE CHALLENGES AND REQUESTS TO PERFORM

Every now and then you will meet someone who thinks it would be loads of laughs for you to perform like a circus act.

Perhaps they have an idle curiosity to satisfy. They ask—even insist—upon some demonstration of your talent on the spot. "Can you read my aura right now?" "Should I sell such-and-such a stock?" "What did I eat for lunch last Tuesday?" "What's the winning lottery number?" Treating these flippant requests seriously will only drain your energy and invite more of the same.

Deflect them with something like, "I don't think this is the appropriate place/time/forum for that . . ." or "Sorry, I'm off duty now." It serves no useful purpose, to you, your gift or to anyone present, to jump because someone insists. Once during the intermission of a lecture, a young man said to me, "What am I thinking right now?" I replied with a smile, "You're wondering whether or not I can tell what you're thinking," and I changed the subject. If you offer intuitive consultations on a professional basis, you can say, "If you're interested in a consultation, I'd be happy to discuss how I work and set up an appointment."

Occasionally you will run into an out-and-out skeptic—who is likely to be hostile as well—who will demand a demonstration to prove you have an ability. Nothing will make a skeptic happy, and anything you offer will be used as more grist for grinding you down.

DECLINE HEALTH MATTERS

Without a medical license, it is against the law to make medical diagnoses. Do not do so. Period. There is a growing profession of "medical intuitives" who train under a doctor's supervision to act as consultants in medical matters. If using your intuitive ability in the health care professions appeals to you, investigate this type of training. There also are many training programs in energy healing, though these still do not qualify you to make medical diagnoses.

Above all, *never* predict if or when somebody—or a pet either—is going to die. You could create a nightmare for that person and others. The time of death is between each soul and the Creator. Forces in motion change moment to moment. No matter what you might intuit at any given time, you may not be seeing the whole picture.

Once a psychic, whom I was consulting for a reading, volunteered out of the blue, and rather matter-of-factly, that one of my beloved dogs was soon to die, probably from being hit by a car. I was in a terrible state of anxiety for months. Nothing happened. The dog lived for another 10 years and died of old age. Such a reading lacked both responsibility and consideration.

Readings and Consultations

Many people who develop their intuitive ability go on to give readings and consultations on a professional basis, charging fees for their services. If you wish to become a reader, pay special attention to the foregoing etiquette.

When people seek out a reading, they look upon the reader as an authority. Negative comments and pronouncements can have a devastating effect. This doesn't mean that a reader should paint a false, rosy picture. Just be sensitive to how things are worded.

Most people get readings because they have problems they wish to solve. A reading should be constructive and empowering. It is not a substitute for professional counseling or therapy. Remind your clients of this.

It's a good idea to make a statement at the beginning of a session that sets out the parameters of the reading. When I gave readings, I told people that the purpose of a reading was to provide insight that would help them make their own decisions. I stressed that any impressions of future outcomes were based on forces in motion, and could change as people changed their intent and actions. We have free will.

Readings have been outlawed in many places in the past, and even today laws can vary considerably. In the U.S., for example, some states allow readings only for "entertainment purposes," and this purpose must clearly be stated by the practitioners. Familiarize yourself with your local laws.

There are always going to be some people who want readers to tell them what they should do about everything, big and small, going on in their life. I don't encourage dependency on readings.

If you give readings, you will find that some go very well and others are a struggle. We simply tune in to people differently. You might find that your own intuition will guide you in this matter. When someone asks for a reading, you will know whether or not you should give one. You may not be the right person for them; or, they may want you to tell them something that you really can't guarantee. There's nothing wrong with declining a reading. Gently, of course.

If you have a genuine desire to help people, and you ask your Higher Self to guide you accordingly, you are likely to be a successful reader.

ESP Cards

ESP cards and practice kits can be obtained from:

The Institute for Parapsychology
Rhine Research Center
402 North Buchanan Blvd.
Durham, NC 27701
Phone: 919-688-8241

Endnotes

CHAPTER 1: INTUITION IS YOUR BIRTHRIGHT

1. Little, Alan, "How I Stopped Nuclear War," BBC website, www.news.bbc.co.uk. October 21, 1998.
2. Guiley, Rosemary Ellen, *Harper's Encyclopedia of Mystical and Paranormal Experience*, (San Francisco: HarperSanFrancisco, 1991), p. 466.

CHAPTER 3: INTUITION SPEAK

1. Schulz, Mona Lisa, *Awakening Intuition: Using Your Mind-Body Network for Insight and Healing*, (New York: Harmony Books, 1998), pp. 17–18.
2. Briggs, John, *Fire in the Crucible: The Alchemy of Creative Genius*, (New York: St. Martin's Press, 1988), p. 40.
3. Guiley, Rosemary Ellen, *Angels of Mercy*, (New York: Pocket Books, 1994), pp. 86–87.
4. Dyer, Wayne W., *Real Magic: Creating Miracles in Everyday Life*, (New York: HarperCollins, 1992), p. 69.
5. Guiley, Rosemary Ellen, *Harper's Encyclopedia of Mystical and Paranormal Experience, op. cit.*, p. 287.

6. _____, *Forever Love: How to Find Your Soul Mate*, copyright 1998.

7. Adrienne, Carol, *The Purpose of Your Life*, (New York: William Morrow & Company, 1998), p. 24.

8. *Ibid.*, p. 108.

9. Greatrex, Derek, "A Note on Synchronicity and Seriality," *Paranormal Review*, Issue 9, January 1999, p. 5.

10. Levoy, Gregg, *Callings: Finding and Following an Authentic Life*, (New York: Harmony Books, 1997), pp. 109–110.

CHAPTER 4: OPENING YOUR INTUITION GATE

1. Guiley, Rosemary Ellen, *The Miracle of Prayer: True Stories of Blessed Healing*, (New York: Pocket Books, 1995), p. 66.

2. Kelly, Katy, "A lifetime spent romancing stones pays off in green," *USA Today*, March 16, 1999, p. 10D.

3. Palmer, Helen, ed. *Inner Knowing* (New York: Jeremy P. Tarcher/Putnam, 1998), p. 129.

4. Guiley, Rosemary Ellen, *Angels of Mercy, op. cit.*, pp. 121–122.

CHAPTER 5: COSMIC CONNECTIONS

1. Radin, Dean I., *The Conscious Universe: The Scientific Truth of Psychic Phenomena*, (San Francisco: HarperEdge, 1997), p. 172.

2. Miller 149

3. Ornstein, Robert, *The Evolution of Consciousness*, (New York: Prentice Hall Press, 1991), p. 277.

4. Russell, Peter, *Waking Up in Time: Finding Inner Peace in Times of Accelerating Change*, (Novato, Calif.: Origin Press, 1998), p. 154.

5. For details about these studies, see *Executive ESP* by Douglas Dean, John Mihalasky, Sheila Ostrander, and Lynn Schroeder; Englewood Cliffs, N.J.: Prentice Hall, 1974.

6. Guiley, Rosemary Ellen, *Harper's Encyclopedia of Mystical and Paranormal Experience, op. cit.,* p. 438.

7. Seale, Alan, *On Becoming a 21st-Century Mystic: Pathways to Intuitive Living*, (New York: Skytop Publishing, 1997), p. 21.

8. Naparstek, Belleruth, *Your Sixth Sense: Activating Your Psychic Potential*, (San Francisco: HarperSanFrancisco, 1997), p. xvii.
9. *Ibid.*, p. 5.

CHAPTER 6: THE HOLISTIC INTUITIVE LIFESTYLE

1. Guiley, Rosemary Ellen, *Harper's Encyclopedia of Mystical and Paranormal Experience, op. cit.,* p. 355.
2. For a discussion of scientific studies on prayer, see *Healing Words: The Power of Prayer and the Practice of Medicine* by Larry Dossey, San Francisco: HarperSanFranciso, 1993.
3. Underhill, Evelyn, *Mysticism*, (New York: New American Library, 1974), p. 64.
4. Dyer, Wayne W., *op. cit.*, p. 58.
5. Briggs, John, *op. cit.*, pp. 63–64.
6. Underhill, Evelyn, *op. cit.*, p. 64.
7. Campbell, Don, *The Mozart Effect*, (New York: Avon Books, 1997), p. 27.

KEY #5: EXPANDED VISION

1. Tenshin, Okakura, *The Book of Tea*, (Tokyo: Kodansha International, 1998), p. 147.

KEY #6: EXPANDED LISTENING

1. Steiner, Rudolph, *How to Know Higher Worlds*, (Hudson, N.Y.: Anthroposophic Press, 1994), pp. 47–48.

KEY #12: THE DREAM ORACLE

1. Guiley, Rosemary Ellen, *Harper's Encyclopedia of Mystical and Paranormal Experience, op. cit.*, p. 185.

KEY #17: HIDE-AND-SEEK

1. Interview with author.

CHAPTER 8: GETTING THE MESSAGE

1. Northrup, Christiane, *Women's Bodies, Women's Wisdom*, (New York: Bantam Books, 1994), p. 59.

CHAPTER 9: PROBLEM SOLVING AND DECISION MAKING

1. Guiley, Rosemary Ellen, *Angels of Mercy, op. cit.*, pp. 112–113.

CHAPTER 10: FINDING YOUR PURPOSE AND ACHIEVING GOALS

1. Peale, Norman Vincent, *The Power of Positive Thinking*, (New York: Prentice Hall, 1952), p. 56.

CHAPTER 13: ENHANCING YOUR CREATIVITY, HEALTH, AND SELF-IMPROVEMENT

1. Sherman, Harold, *How to Make ESP Work for You*, (Los Angeles: DeVorss & Company, 1964), p. 83.
2. *Ibid.*, p. 84.
3. Adapted from *Inner Visioning: Inspired Insights for Creative Living and Leadership*, copyright Toni G. Boehm and Rosemary Ellen Guiley.
4. Weil, Andrew, *Spontaneous Healing*, (New York: Alfred A. Knopf, 1995), p. 193.
5. Borysenko Joan, and Miroslav Borysenko, *The Power of the Mind to Heal*, (Carson, Calif.: Hay House, 1994), pp. 64–65.
6. For a discussion of the role of dreams in healing, see *Dreamwork for the Soul* by Rosemary Ellen Guiley, New York: Berkley Books, 1998.
7. Guiley, Rosemary Ellen, *I Bring You Glad Tidings*, New York: Pocket Books, in press.

Bibliography

Adams, Scott. *The Dilbert Future: Thriving on Business Stupidity in the 21st Century*. New York: HarperBusiness, 1998.

Adrienne, Carol. *The Purpose of Your Life*. New York: William Morrow & Company, 1998.

Artress, Lauren. *Walking a Sacred Path: Rediscovering the Labyrinth As a Sacred Tool*. New York: Riverheard Books, 1995.

Beasley, Victor R. *Intuition by Design: Applying Your Intuitive Intelligence for Personal and Business Decision-Making*. Livermore, Calif.: Oughten House Publications, 1995.

Belitz, Charlene and Meg Lundstrom. *The Power of Flow: Practical Ways to Transform Your Life with Meaningful Coincidence*. New York: Harmony Books, 1997.

Borysenko, Joan and Miroslav Borysenko. *The Power of the Mind to Heal*. Carson, Calif.: Hay House, 1994.

Briggs, John. *Fire in the Crucible: The Alchemy of Creative Genius*. New York: St. Martin's Press, 1988.

Campbell, Don. *The Mozart Effect*. New York: Avon Books, 1997.

Choquette, Sonia. *Your Heart's Desire: Instructions for Creating the Life You Really Want*. New York: Three Rivers Press, 1997.

Csikszentmihalyi, Mihaly. *Flow: The Psychology of Optimal Experience*. New York: HarperCollins, 1990.

Dean, Douglas and John Mihalasky and Sheila Ostrander and Lynn Schroeder. *Executive ESP*. Englewood Cliffs, N.J.: Prentice Hall, 1974.

Dossey, Larry. *Healing Words: The Power of Prayer and the Practice of Medicine*. San Francisco: HarperSanFranciso, 1993.

Dyer, Wayne W. *Real Magic: Creating Miracles in Everyday Life*. New York: HarperCollins, 1992.

Einstein, Patricia. *Intuition: Path to Inner Wisdom*. Rockport, Mass.: Element Books, 1997.

Emery, Marcia. *Intuition Workbook: An Expert's Guide to Unlocking the Wisdom of Your Subconscious Mind*. Englewood Cliffs, N.J.: Prentice Hall, 1994.

Gawain, Shakti. *Creative Visualization*. New York: Bantam Books, 1982.

Greatrex, Derek, "A Note on Synchronicity and Seriality," *Paranormal Review*, Issue 9, January 1999, p. 5.

Guiley, Rosemary Ellen. *Harper's Encyclopedia of Mystical and Paranormal Phenomena*. San Francisco: HarperSanFrancisco, 1991.

―――. *Angels of Mercy*. New York: Pocket Books, 1994.

―――. *The Miracle of Prayer: True Stories of Blessed Healing*. New York: Pocket Books, 1995.

―――. *Dreamwork for the Soul*. New York: Berkley Books, 1998.

Harman, Willis. *Global Mind Change*. Sausalito, Calif.: Institute of Noetic Sciences, 1998.

―――and Howard Rheingold. *Higher Creativity: Liberating the Unconscious for Breakthrough Insights*. Los Angeles: Jeremy P. Tarcher/Putnam, 1984.

Kelly, Katy. "A lifetime spent romancing stones pays off in green," *USA Today*, March 16, 1999, p. 10D.

Leonard, George and Michael Murphy. *The Life We Are Given*. New York: Jeremy P. Tarcher/Putnam, 1995.

Levoy, Gregg. *Callings: Finding and Following an Authentic Life*. New York: Harmony Books, 1997.

Little, Alan. "How I Stopped Nuclear War," BBC Web site, www.newsbbc.co.uk, October 21, 1998.

Miller, Carolyn. *Creating Miracles: Understanding the Experience of Divine Intervention*. Tiburon, Calif.: HJ Kramer, 1995.

Mishlove, Jeffrey. *The Roots of Consciousness* (rev.). Tulsa: Council Oak Books, 1999.

Moody, Raymond. *Reunions: Visionary Encounters with Departed Loved Ones*. New York: Villard Books, 1993.

Murphy, Michael and Rhea A. White. *In the Zone: Transcendent Experience in Sports*. New York: Penguin Books, 1995.

Naparstek, Belleruth. *Your Sixth Sense: Activating Your Psychic Potential*. San Francisco: HarperSanFrancisco, 1997.

Northrup, Christiane. *Women's Bodies, Women's Wisdom*. New York: Bantam Books, 1994.

Ornstein, Robert. *The Evolution of Consciousness*. New York: Prentice Hall Press, 1991.

Palmer, Helen (ed.). *Inner Knowing*. New York: Jeremy P. Tarcher/Putnam, 1998.

Peale, Norman Vincent. *The Power of Positive Thinking*. New York: Prentice Hall, 1952.

Peirce, Penney. *The Intuitive Way: A Guide to Living from Inner Wisdom*. Hillsboro, Ore.: Beyond Words Publishing, 1997.

Radin, Dean I. *The Conscious Universe: The Scientific Truth of Psychic Phenomena*. San Francisco: Harper*Edge*, 1997.

Remele, Patricia. *Money Freedom: Finding Your Source of Wealth*. Virginia Beach, Va.: ARE Press, 1995.

Rosanoff, Nancy. "Intuitive Investing," *Intuition*, April 1999, pp. 14–21.

———. *Intuition Workout: A Practical Guide to Discovering and Developing Your Inner Knowing*. Boulder Creek, Calif.: Aslan Publishing, 1988.

Russell, Peter. *Waking Up in Time: Finding Inner Peace in Times of Accelerating Change*. Novato, Calif.: Origin Press, 1998.

Satprem. *Sri Aurobindo or the Adventure of Consciousness*. Mt. Vernon, Wash.: Institute for Evolutionary Research, 1993.

Schulz, Mona Lisa. *Awakening Intuition: Using Your Mind-Body Network for Insight and Healing*. New York: Harmony Books, 1998.

Seale, Alan. *On Becoming a 21st-Century Mystic: Pathways to Intuitive Living*. New York: Skytop Publishing, 1997.

Sherman, Harold. *How to Make ESP Work for You*. Los Angeles: DeVorss & Company, 1964.

Smoley, Richard. "Divining for Dollars," *Intuition*, August 1998, pp. 24–29+.

Spangler, David. *Everyday Miracles: The Inner Art of Manifestation*. New York: Bantam Books, 1996.

Steiner, Rudolph. *How to Know Higher Worlds*. Hudson, N.Y.: Anthroposophic Press, 1994.

Stover, Walt. "Precognitive Dreams for Prosperity and Abundance," *Dream Network,* Vol. 18 No. 2, pp. 42–43.

Suzuki, Shunryu. *Zen Mind, Beginner's Mind*. New York: Weatherhill, 1970.

Tenshin, Okakura. *The Book of Tea*. Tokyo: Kodansha International, 1998.

Underhill, Evelyn. *Mysticism*. New York: New American Library, 1974.

Vaughn, Frances E. *Awakening Intuition*. Garden City, N.Y.: Anchor Books, 1979.

Weil, Andrew. *Spontaneous Healing*. New York: Alfred A. Knopf, 1995.

About the Author

ROSEMARY ELLEN GUILEY IS A BESTSELLING AUTHOR ON dreams, intuition, and visionary experience. She is president of her own company, Visionary Living, Inc., based in Arnold, Maryland, a provider of inspirational and practical resources for enhancement in personal growth, creativity, relationships, and work. Rosemary has written more than twenty books on a variety of subjects, published around the world. Visit her Web site, www.visionaryliving.com, to find out more about Rosemary's work, books, and tapes, her speaking and media schedule and other news.

Visionaryliving.com features a library of articles on dreams, intuition, prayer, healing, self-improvement, and other subjects. You are invited to register to receive a complimentary monthly e-column.